THE UNBREAKABLE HUMAN SPIRIT OF RESILIENCE

THE UNBREAKABLE HUMAN SPIRIT OF RESILIENCE

A Boy's Journey from Adversity to Triumph

DESMOND ERIC KETTER, LPC

Legacy Lantern Publishing House

The Unbreakable Human Spirit of Resilience: A Boy's Journey from Adversity to Triumph
Copyright © 2024 by Desmond Eric Ketter, LPC.
All rights reserved.
Cover Designed By: Abdulqoyum Abiolo
No part of this publication may be reproduced, distributed, or transmitted in any form or by any means, including photocopying, recording, or other electronic or mechanical methods, without the prior written permission of the author or publisher, except in the case of brief quotations embodied in critical reviews and certain other noncommercial uses permitted by copyright law.
Published by Legacy Lantern Publishing House.
Publisher's Note: This book is a work of non-fiction. While it recounts true events from the author's life, certain names, characters, businesses, places, events, locales, and incidents have been altered or used fictitiously to preserve privacy and protect individual identities. Any resemblance to actual persons, living or dead, or actual events, is purely coincidental and not intended by the author.
For permission requests, write or email to the publisher, addressed "Attention: Permissions Coordinator," at the address below.
Legacy Lantern Publishing House, LLC
2108 N St, Suite C
Sacramento, CA 95816
support@legacylanternpublishing.com
LIBRARY OF CONGRESS CATALOGING-IN-PUBLICATION DATA
Names: Ketter, Desmond Eric, author.
Title: The Unbreakable Human Spirit of Resilience: A Boy's Journey from Adversity to Triumph / Desmond Eric Ketter, LPC.
Description: Sacramento: Legacy Lantern Publishing House, 2024 | Includes bibliographical references.
Identifiers: ISBN 979-8-9905578-0-2 (paperback- print) | ISBN 979-8-9905578-3-3 (hardcovers- print)
ISBN 979-8-9905578-2-6 (ebook)
Subjects: BISAC BIO026000 BIOGRAPHY & AUTOBIOGRAPHY / Personal Memoirs.
Classification: (LCC) CT275.K47 A3 2024 | DDC [Fic] 920.72—dc23
ISBN: 979-8-9905578-3-3
Printed in the United States of America
First Edition

ADVANCE PRAISE FOR THE UNBREAKABLE HUMAN SPIRIT OF RESILIENCE

"Desmond Ketter's new book, 'The Unbreakable Human Spirit of Resilience: A Boy's Journey from Adversity to Triumph' is an interesting read, filled with exhilarating information that is bound to keep the attention of the most avid reader. This book explores Desmond's childhood and young adult experience in Liberia under many challenging circumstances and the destined opportunity for him and his family to relocate timely to the United States. The effective storytelling skills of the author are certain to keep readers captivated and hungry for more adventurous tales as tests and trials providentially turn to triumphs. This book is about hope and victory amid relentless life challenges. I strongly endorse the book for its depth of information, unique content, and clear writing style."

—Dr. Paul Okoruwa, Oral Roberts University and President of African Christian Fellowship, Tulsa, Oklahoma Chapter

"I'm so proud of everything Desmond has done to advance his life to this successful and fulfilling point. His story is enthralling—from the war-torn streets of Liberia to the academic hallways of America. Sapulpa Public Schools is lucky to have him."

— Karen Gaddis, Former Teacher and Counselor, Former State Representative

"This is the story of how Desmond answered the call of God and how faith enabled him to overcome challenges and difficulties to emerge stronger and more fulfilled as a person. It is the story of one person, but in his story our lessons that can be adapted by each of us to enrich our own lives by answering God's calling."

—Rodger A. Randle, Professor and Director of the Center for

Studies in Democracy and Culture, University of Oklahoma, British Honorary Consul of Oklahoma, and Former Mayor of Tulsa

"Over the Easter weekend, while visiting my elderly parents, I found myself deeply engrossed in 'The Unbreakable Human Spirit of Resilience.' My curiosity caught the attention of my dad, a retired history professor, who, intrigued by the sight of the printed copy I had brought along, began asking about it. Although I had not yet finished, I shared the essence of Desmond's remarkable journey with him as best as I could. His immediate curiosity and genuine interest in reading the memoir is a testament to the book's compelling narrative and universal appeal."

—Jody Worley, Ph.D., Associate Professor and Doctoral Program Coordinator for Organizational and Community Leadership, University of Oklahoma

To my adored late grandmother, Ma Kumba Saah Sakawolo, and my beloved mother, Mrs. Doris Tamba Ayeni. In life's storms, you were my lighthouse, guiding me toward my dreams with your eternal flame. This book honors you, two pillars of resilience and love, who shaped an ordinary boy into a man capable of change. Your spirits light my path and echo in every word written on these pages. Through me, you both continue to light the path for countless others.

I love you both.

Contents

Dedication   vii
Foreword   xi
Epigraph   xv
Prologue   xvi
Preface   xviii
Introduction   xx

THE SEEDS OF ADVERSITY

1   The Echoes of Childhood   2
2   Under the Shadow of War   31

THE JOURNEY TO HOPE

3   A New Dawn   80
4   The Guiding Light   85

THE POWER OF TRANSFORMATION

5   Turning Pages   102
6   The Seed of Change   132
7   Rising from the Ashes   147

8	Lighting the Path	153
9	The Power of Pen	160
10	The Promise Fulfilled	167
11	The Journey Continues	175
Conclusion		177

Epilogue — 181
Afterword — 183
Acknowledgements — 185
Index — 188
Notes — 189
References — 191
About The Author — 192

Foreword

In the tapestry of human existence, woven with threads of triumph and despair, joy and hardship, there exists a universal narrative—the resilience of the human spirit. It is a narrative that transcends borders, cultures, and circumstances, binding us together in our shared journey of growth, transformation, and triumph. "The Unbreakable Human Spirit of Resilience" is a poignant memoir that delves deep into the heart of this narrative, offering readers a glimpse into the indomitable strength that resides within each of us.

I have the profound honor of knowing Mr. Desmond Ketter during his tenure in the University of Oklahoma's Clinical Mental Health Counseling program. He excelled in his studies which emphasized trauma and strategies for healing trauma. I witnessed firsthand the strength, intelligence, courage, faith, and resilience forged within him from his loving family, his rich cultural heritage, and his rigorous journey through pain and suffering. His successes have been hard fought and justly deserved. Now he is blessed with a blossoming career, a beautiful family, a supportive community, and the completion of this inspiring book.

As I embarked on this cathartic journey through

the pages of this memoir, I was struck by the raw openness and vulnerability that memoir-writing demands. The Mr. Ketter's courage in laying bare the wounds of the past, once carefully hidden beneath a veneer of strength, is a testament to the transformative power of storytelling. Each memory revisited in these pages is a ghost resurrected, a reminder of the resilience that carried the author through the darkest of times.

From the rugged streets of Liberia to the scholarly corridors of Oklahoma, the Mr. Ketter's journey is a testament to the human spirit's capacity to rise from the ashes of despair and forge a path towards transformation. Through the author's eyes, we witness the tumultuous landscapes of war, cultural transition, and personal growth, each chapter a testament to the resilience that propels us forward in the face of adversity.

One of the central themes that resonates throughout this memoir is the profound impact of guidance and support in times of need. The author's grandmother and mother emerge as beacons of strength, imparting wisdom, love, and resilience that shape his journey towards triumph. Their legacy of resilience and sacrifice serves as a guiding light, illuminating the path through darkness and instilling in the author a deep sense of cultural identity and familial heritage. This story reminds of these truths: No one gets through this life alone. We survive and flourish through our connections with significant others throughout our lives. We are indebted to our families, our cultures, and our ancestors for their courage, resilience, love, and wisdom in paving the roads before us.

As Mr. Ketter navigates the complexities of trauma and loss during the First Liberian Civil War, readers are invited to glean valuable insights into coping mechanisms for trauma and Post-Traumatic Stress Disorder (PTSD). Through the author's experiences, we learn about the transformative power of writing as therapy, the resilience that acts as a protective factor against PTSD, and the importance of support systems in fostering healing and strength.

The author's reflections on empathy, healing, and the reframing of trauma offer a profound understanding of the human capacity to endure, grow, and triumph in the face of unimaginable challenges. By sharing his story and shedding light on the realities of war, the author extends a hand of empathy to readers, inviting them to join him on a journey of resilience, courage, and transformation.

In the pages that follow, readers will discover a narrative that transcends individual experiences to touch upon the universal themes of resilience, courage, and transformation. It is a narrative that speaks to the shared human experience of struggle, triumph, learning, and growth—a narrative that reminds us of the unbreakable spirit that resides within each of us, waiting to be awakened in times of need.

As you embark on this journey through the pages

of "The Unbreakable Human Spirit of Resilience," may you find inspiration, solace, and courage in the author's words. May you be reminded of the strength that lies within you, waiting to be unleashed in the face of adversity. And may you carry forward the lessons of resilience, empathy, and transformation found within these pages, weaving them into the tapestry of your own unique journey towards triumph.

With each word read, may you feel the echoes of resilience reverberating within you, guiding you towards a deeper understanding of the unbreakable human spirit that resides within us all.

Chad V. Johnson, Ph.D.
The University of Oklahoma
Tulsa, OK

Epigraph

"WHAT LIES BEHIND US AND WHAT LIES BEFORE US ARE
TINY MATTERS COMPARED TO WHAT LIES WITHIN US."
– RALPH WALDO EMERSON

Prologue

In the heart of the African continent, cradled in the hands of the Atlantic, there is a land baptized by the duality of man. A land of exquisite beauty yet marked by the scars of human conflict. It is here, in the lush green jungles and the warm, golden sands of Liberia, where my story is rooted.

Liberia, Latin for "the land of the free," has been both my haven and battlefield, the cradle of my existence and the crucible of my resilience. A nation born out of the quest for liberty, it came to be the theater of two devastating civil wars, leaving its soil soaked in innocent blood, its air echoing with cries of despair. Yet, amidst the chaos and pain, it was in Liberia where I first experienced the invincible strength of the human spirit.

My home was where life's sweetest moments were cradled in the same arms that bore its harshest realities; a contradiction that lent our existence a poignant, soul-stirring depth. It was where each sunrise carried the promise of survival, and every sunset sang tales of our unyielding resilience.

Life unfolded in the bustling, vibrant district of West Point, known for its rampant crime but celebrated for its strong sense of community. The spirit of the place captured in the saying "If you make it out of West Point, you can make it anywhere," molded me and guided me through life's challenges.

It was a tale of two cities within me. One, a child born in the throes of ceaseless conflict, where dreams were cloaked in the harsh realities of survival. The other, is a determined spirit, refusing to be defined by circumstance, aiming to transcend the turmoil and strive for a life beyond the confines of the infamous West Point.

This memoir is more than a chronicle of my journey; it's a testament to the tenacity of the human spirit that blooms amidst adversity. It is a narrative of survival, resilience, and triumph, played against the vivid backdrop of Liberia's chaotic past.

In sharing my story, I aim to illuminate the echoes of resilience that resonate in every corner of West Point, the lessons of survival imprinted on the sands of Liberia, and the spirit of freedom that lives within us all. Above all, I hope to reveal the undying essence of Liberia—a nation of survivors, of fighters, of dreamers who, even in the face of daunting challenges, refuse to be extinguished.

Come journey with me...through the bustling streets of West Point, along the winding road to liberation, into the heart of the land that shaped me. Let's embark on this journey together, for it is in the telling and the hearing of these stories, in the sharing of our struggles and triumphs, that we truly make sense of our existence. So, as we delve into the pages of the past, may we also uncover the promise of a brighter future, not just for me, but for Liberia, and the world. Because if you make it out of West Point, you can make it anywhere.

This is my story. The story of a boy from Liberia who dared to dream. This is my journey, my shifts, my transformation, my triumph, my promise. Welcome to my world, a world where adversity fuels the journey toward success. Let's begin the journey.

Preface

In the web of life, we each tread our unique paths, marked by moments of triumph and times of despair, peaks of joy, and valleys of hardship. Our experiences shape us, our struggles test us, and our victories inspire us. Yet, amidst this diverse tapestry of human experience, there lies a universal thread—the resilience of the human spirit.

"The Unbreakable Human Spirit of Resilience: A Boy's Journey from Adversity to Triumph" invites you on a profound journey alongside me. This narrative transcends mere recounting of events, delving deep into lessons harvested from life's fiercest battlegrounds—a celebration of the unyielding spirit dwelling within us all.

Rooted in the harsh reality of growing up in Liberia's war-torn streets and transitioning through the vast cultural landscape of the United States, my lived experience unfolds. This tale of resilience, refined through challenges of assimilation, education, and relentless pursuit of personal growth, finds its inspiration during sleepless nights spent with my daughter, Noelle Kumba, named after my late grandmother. Reflecting on my transformative journey from past to present inspired me to share this story.

Addressing the universal challenge of confronting life's adversities, this book aims to demonstrate that resilience is a tangible reality. It is a testament to the notion that our past chapters do not confine us; rather, they lay the foundation upon which we can construct a future filled with hope and determination.

More than an individual story, this memoir mirrors the shared human experience—struggle, triumph, learning, and growth. It celebrates the spirit that refuses to be defined by circumstances, that finds strength in each challenge, propelling us toward transformation.

As you delve into these pages, my hope is that you'll not only understand my journey but also feel empowered to embrace and author your own story of resilience. This journey is an invitation to celebrate the resilience that defines us, to resonate with my experiences, and to recognize fragments of your own story within mine.

Thank you for joining me on this voyage through "The Unbreakable Human Spirit of Resilience." Together, let's explore the therapeutic power of storytelling, the solace in shared experiences, and the transformative potential of resilience. As we conclude this preface, remember: your story is still unfolding. Let it be a testament to your resilience, a reflection of your strength, and a beacon of hope for others.

Here's to our unbreakable spirits, to the stories we share, and to the chapters yet unwritten. I'm ready to take this journey—are you? Let's begin.

Introduction

"The Unbreakable Human Spirit of Resilience: A Boy's Journey from Adversity to Triumph" delves into what readers can expect to discover within its pages. This memoir transcends a simple recounting of events; it's an in-depth exploration of resilience, a journey through adversity, and ultimately, a celebration of triumph against all odds. Offering both my personal narrative and universal lessons, this book illuminates the power of the human spirit to overcome seemingly impossible challenges.

Resilience, the capacity to adapt or recover from adversities, is a central theme woven throughout the story. It aims to dissect the anatomy of resilience, showcasing how it emerges not only in the face of physical and emotional challenges but also through cultural assimilation, educational pursuits, and professional development. My journey from the war-torn streets of Liberia to my role as a mental health counselor and therapist in the United States provides a firsthand look at resilience in action.

For you, the reader, this book offers insights into the transformative power of resilience. You'll learn how adversity can act as a catalyst for personal growth and how the support of loved ones can provide the strength to persevere. Designed to inspire those facing their own struggles, this book provides hope and demonstrates that it's possible to rise from despair to success and fulfillment.

Furthermore, this narrative emphasizes the significance of embracing our past not as a limitation but as a chapter in our ongoing story. It affirms that we are the authors of our lives, capable of rewriting our destinies with resilience as our guide.

My aim is to engage with you on a journey of reflection and inspiration. "The Unbreakable Human Spirit of Resilience" serves as a companion in your exploration of resilience, offering a narrative that not only resonates with your personal experiences but also empowers you to envision and strive for a triumphant future.

The Seeds of Adversity

In my early years, amidst Liberia's turmoil, I found the seeds of resilience. This part recounts my childhood trials and my family's legacy, laying the foundation for my unbreakable spirit and the journey that would unfold from the soil of adversity.

I

The Echoes of Childhood

"IT IS EASIER TO BUILD STRONG CHILDREN THAN TO REPAIR BROKEN MEN." – FREDERICK DOUGLASS

In Liberia, whispers of resilience and pain mingle within the rich red soil. This, dear reader, is where my journey begins—a testament to endurance, forever marked by the haunting echoes of civil war. West Point, or as my father lovingly called it, "Keys," serves as the backdrop of my early years—a paradox of vibrancy and peril nestled within the bustling heart of Monrovia. Here, amidst the palpable fear, a resilient sense of community blossomed.

In West Point, laughter danced alongside crime, permeating both the air and the homes of families who defiantly sought joy amidst adversity. Here, "gronnahs" ceased to be mere words; they embodied individuals like us—those who, devoid of conventional parental guidance, defied the odds and flourished.

The roots of West Point stretch back to the Kru and Bassa fishermen and traders, drawn by the promise of prosperity beneath the looming skyline of downtown Monrovia. Over time, it flourished into a fortress of tenacity, a testament to the strong spirit of those yearning to carve their destiny away from the gaze of the privileged few. The adage, "If you make it out of West Point, you can make it anywhere," resonated deeply within me—not merely a saying, but an emotional reminder of our shared strength and resilience.

In the fabric of my childhood, my grandparents emerged as strong figures, embodying the resilience demanded by life in West Point. Grandmother Kumba, our family's steadfast matriarch, wove through the vibrant markets, ensuring our sustenance amid the struggle. Meanwhile, Grandfather Isaac, a man of considerable influence, left behind a legacy that proved both a blessing and a curse. His unconventional choice to bestow upon my father the 'Ketter' surname deviated from tradition, weaving a tapestry of identity complexities that puzzled me for years.

I soon came to understand the deep gap wealth could create, a divide often widened by the destructive forces of greed and betrayal, overshadowing even the strongest of family bonds. My parents, humble traders navigating the risky currents of fortune, confronted these adversities with unwavering determination, transforming each modest meal into a triumph over adversity. Yet, the presence of greedy relatives and the deceitfulness of a woman once embraced as kin by my grandfather cast a dark wall over our existence, infusing our lives with additional layers of turmoil.

Amidst this turbulent era, characterized by both personal and communal turmoil, the instability of our existence became painfully evident. Yet, amidst the chaos, my grandfather's home near the serene Montserrado River stood as a steadfast beacon of hope, tying me to a past woven with threads of both joy and struggle. Our humble backyard was repurposed into an impromptu soccer field, and the nearby stretch of the Atlantic Ocean emerged as the backdrop to a childhood defined by unwavering resilience and unyielding defiance.

Amidst the betrayals and mysterious family secrets covering my grandfather's lineage, the undefeated spirit of West Point left a permanent imprint on my character. Despite its inherent dangers and persistent trials, the crucible of West Point became the forge where my resilience was strengthened. This chapter serves as a tribute to those transformative years, commemorating the legacy that sculpted me, the intricate tapestry of family bonds, and the unwavering spirit of a community that imparted upon me the profound meaning of resilience.

As I came of age in Liberia, a nation entrenched in the arduous quest for freedom amid relentless turmoil, every passing day bore witness to the resilience of the human spirit. The ceaseless battle for fundamental human rights—security, provisions, shelter—remained a vague aspiration for countless souls. Yet, amidst this intricate composition of hardship, a universal symphony unfolded, transcending the boundaries of faith, age, and social standing. In our collective struggle, we discovered solace in solidarity, and in the unwavering belief that each dawn revealed the promise of renewal and possibility.

I emerged into the world and was nurtured amidst the vibrant embrace of West Point, affectionately known as "Keys" by my father. Nestled as a densely populated peninsula between the Montserrado and Saint Paul rivers, caressed by the Atlantic's salty breeze, Keys boasted a captivating duality. Despite its reputation for increasing crime, it held a revered status for its tightly-knit communal ethos—a haven where the resounding echoes of laughter harmonized with the bustling streets. Here, amidst the ceaseless chatter of children playing on sandy shores and the harmonious bustle of family bonds, crime became a mere backdrop against the vibrant scene of communal life.

To those beyond our region, West Point often appeared as a realm inhabited by "gronnahs"—a term rooted in the notion of "grown-up child" within Liberian English or colloquialism. Gronnahs, emblematic of individuals raised without the guiding presence of parental or adult figures, often found themselves navigating the streets alone. Yet, within the heart of West Point, this label transcended its literal meaning, transforming into a poignant symbol of our collective resilience and perseverance.

Amid bustling West Point, my grandparents stood as towering figures of strength and respect. Grandmother Kumba embodied feminine resilience, dedicating herself to petty trading to provide for our family's needs. From the vibrant chaos of the general market, she sold essentials like bitter balls, peppers, okra, and palm oil—products sourced from her birthplace in Lofa County

Grandfather Isaac, with roots in the Gibi-Bassa community of Magibi, was a remarkable presence. Embraced warmly by the Kpelle people, he was bestowed with the name "Ketter," signifying 'big or large'—a name I later adopted as my surname. His career with the Ministry of Public Works enabled him to acquire multiple properties, overseeing the construction of roads, government buildings, and other infrastructure. This provided him with substantial income, allowing him to purchase land and construct a spacious home in West Point for our family. Among his assets was a notable rubber farm in rural Liberia.

One story my mother often recounts is when, as a baby gravely ill, my grandparents took me to one of Grandfather Isaac's rubber farm properties to seek treatment from a local healer.

The mystery surrounding my father's surname, "Ketter," instead of his biological name, "Saywrah," has long puzzled me. Curiously, my grandfather, too, opted not to use his biological surname, instead embracing "James," a tender homage to his older brother who played an important role in his upbringing. According to my father's recollections, his uncle assumed a would-be paternal role, instilling in my grandfather a deep sense of gratitude and affection. Despite the passage of time, the rationale behind these naming choices remains wrapped in mystery, leaving me to ponder their significance to this day.

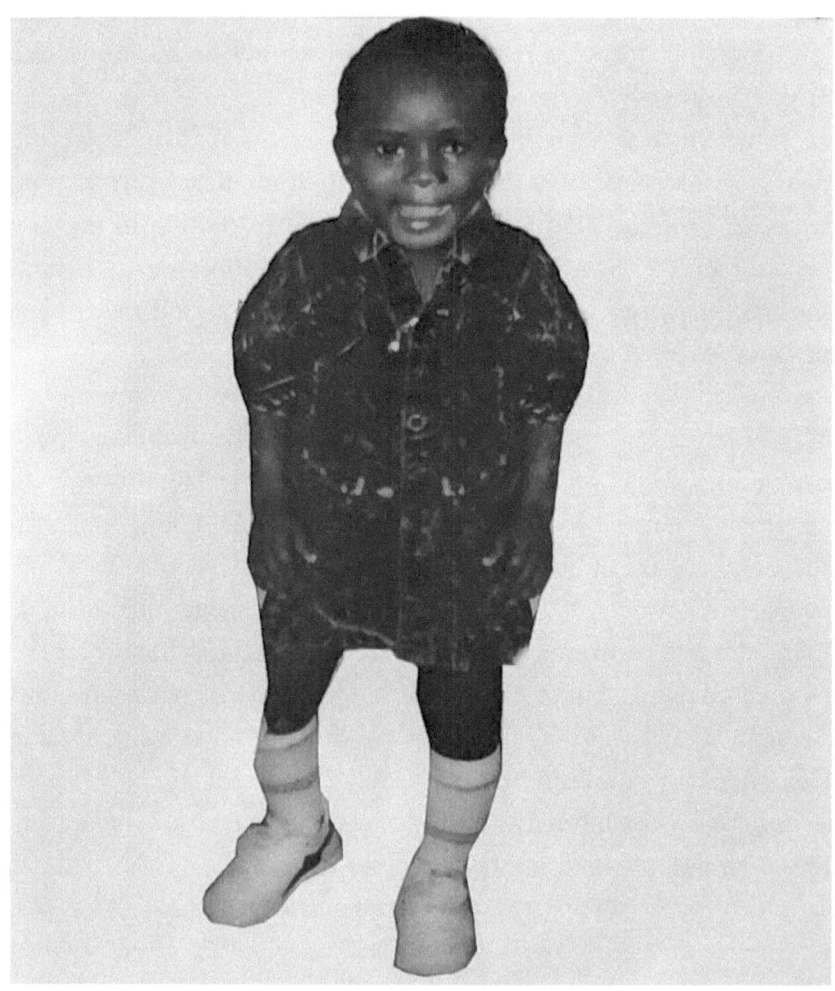

Desmond / Ericboy at 2 years old.

Born into the lineage of my father, I found myself intricately entangled with the profound legacy of my grandfather, evident in the vast expanse of properties he held across Liberia. However, this wealth did not flow down the branches of our family tree as one might assume. Instead, a web of kinship ruined by greed and deceit safeguarded an uneven distribution of this inheritance. While my parents, humble traders in their own right, tirelessly labored to sustain our family, the shadow of inequality loomed large. My mother, a strong businesswoman, sold groceries at the local market—bitter balls, peppers, okra, palm oil, and more—while my father sold shoes and second-hand clothes, affectionately known as 'Dogaflag' in the Liberian dialect. I fondly recall joining them at their market stalls after school, enjoying the simplicity of shared moments over 'Cobowl'—local street food—a cherished tradition that carved unforgettable memories into the fabric of our lives.

Yet, amidst these moments of warmth and companionship, a dark feeling pounded beneath the surface. Opportunistic relatives, driven by my grandfather's ailing health, seized upon our weaknesses, casting our nights into an unending depth of turmoil that stubbornly resisted the arrival of dawn.

A haunting chapter in my life unfolded with my grandfather's illness, serving as the catalyst that upheaved the very foundation of my existence. As his health declined, our nights transformed into battlegrounds of torment, plagued by feverish nightmares that shattered any trace of peacefulness. The once towering figure of my grandfather, representing strength and vitality, now withered before our eyes, caught by the weakness of his mortality, clinging desperately to the fragile thread of life. In the suffocating shadow of his deteriorating health, profound darkness enveloped our family, casting a cloud that seemed to defy the reach of even the faintest glimmer of hope.

In wartime turmoil, a shocking truth emerged: the individual my grandfather once helped with illness conspired with his adopted son to eliminate my father and siblings, aiming to claim my grandfather's properties. This betrayal unfolded after my grandfather extended hospitality to them in our West Point home, unaware of their deceitful motives.

Amidst the trials, the resilience of my family's legacy was embodied by my grandfather's home near the Montserrado River. It served as a beacon, offering solace and connection amidst adversity. From its vantage point, we witnessed the bustling activity of the waterside bridge—a tangible link to the city's past and present, alive with the rhythm of life.

Our backyard transformed into a makeshift soccer field, where countless games culminated in laughter-filled dives as the ball occasionally splashed into the river, prompting cheerful retrievals. These carefree moments stood in stark contrast to the peaceful fishing trips with my father or other relatives, where we would sit by the river in peaceful anticipation, waiting to catch some fish.

Our home, like many others along the river, boasted a makeshift bathroom extending over the water—a commonplace yet somehow adventurous feature. Similarly, my grandmother's house, nestled a stone's throw from the Atlantic Ocean, served as the backdrop for our near-daily beach visits, often in defiance of my parents' cautionary warnings about the dangers of drowning. With cunning stealth, we'd bide our time for the rain to provide cover, sneaking away to the beach undetected, heightening the thrill of our adventures. Reflecting now, it's nothing short of miraculous that we emerged from those adventures unharmed.

THE UNBREAKABLE HUMAN SPIRIT OF RESILIENCE ~ 9

Makeshift bathrooms along the Montserrado Riverbank, West Point, Monrovia, Liberia
Getty Images

Despite relocating from West Point to Mamba Point, the magnetic pull of the ocean remained irresistible, attracting me back to its shores time and again to relive the daring experiences of my youth. These memories, combined with both excitement and apprehension, now stand as cherished milestones of my childhood.

The sinister plot orchestrated by the adopted family my grandfather once aided, utilizing "Juju" or African sorcery cast a dark shadow over my childhood. As an innocent child caught in their web of greed and malice, I witnessed firsthand the insidious attempt to undermine my grandmother and father. My father, the cherished first male child of my grandmother and beloved by my grandfather, emerged as a primary target of their plans. This scheme not only sought to destabilize us emotionally and physically but also aimed to seize control of my grandfather's assets upon his passing.

Tragically, their evil plan nearly succeeded. Following my

grandfather's demise, a string of strange tragedies befell all of my grandmother's children who remained in the house. They succumbed to mysterious illnesses or tragic car accidents, one after another, leaving only my father and two of his sisters alive out of the seven siblings. My younger uncle, Daniel, strangely predicted his death as the last to die before the truth behind the conspiracy was exposed.

This turbulent period was marked by both personal and collective disruption, serving as a chilling reminder of the depths of human wickedness and the resilience required to confront such evil.

On her deathbed, a startling confession shattered the layer of family trust, unveiling a meticulously orchestrated plot in which my uncle—my grandfather's adopted son—played a central role. Unrecognized to many, he and my father shared a familial bond as half-brothers, hidden by the profound respect my father held for him, viewing him as an elder sibling. My father often sought his counsel to navigate family challenges, given his stature as the de facto family leader following my grandfather's passing.

The revelation of his involvement in the conspiracy sent shockwaves through our family. My grandfather had nurtured him, even financing his college education—a gesture of generosity never extended to his children. This revelation reframed the series of tragedies that befell us, exposing the depths of betrayal and the sinister plots that had long worsened within our midst.

Each night plunged me into harrowing suffering, tormented by relentless nightmares of a dragon breathing fire. My painful screams pierced the quiet of my grandfather's house, loud through the corridors. Each morning brought no relief; I awoke soaked in sweat; my body consumed by an unexplained fever that defied medical explanation.

Amidst the uncertainty and fear, my mother remained steadfast, refusing to yield to the mystery of my condition. With unwavering faith, she wrapped me in her loving embrace, a guiding light amid darkness. Despite our relentless pursuit of medical expertise, countless doctors failed to unravel the mystery behind my fever and the haunting nightmares that tortured me each night.

In a moment of desperate determination, my mother turned to my father's family, her words echoing with the fierce protectiveness of a lioness shielding her cub. "My son's blood is bitter. No one can harm him without consequences. You may forsake your own, but you shall not lay a hand on mine. He is a gift from God, entrusted to my care. Cease this torment or face the wrath of divine justice," she declared, her voice firm and unwavering.

The bold declaration by my mother marked the end of my nightmares and the mysterious fevers that had troubled me. Yet, her determination didn't stop there. Seeking divine intervention, she sought the counsel of her pastor, who prayed over me. However, following my grandfather's passing, my father, fearful for our safety, made the difficult decision to relocate us from the family home.

The passing of my grandfather was observed with a grand weeklong celebration of his life, attracting a multitude of friends and family who held him in high regard and cherished him deeply. The wake and funeral became profound gatherings, overflowing with neighbors, friends, relatives, colleagues, and even unfamiliar faces drawn to honor his memory. His enduring legacy lived on in the hearts of those who knew him, casting a radiant light that contrasted sharply with the serious shadows that had once enveloped my early years within his household.

In the harsh realities of West Point, life unfolded as a rigorous lesson in survival, an ongoing battle combined with fleeting moments of human fortitude and unity. Despite the adversities, the unbeatable spirit of community and perseverance served as a steadfast source of optimism. From the risky streets of West Point to the path I now walk, my journey echoes not only my resilience but also the unwavering strength of Liberia itself.

Entangled within the intricate fabric of societal norms and hierarchical constraints, our journey in West Point was fraught with challenges. Yet, as residents of this resilient community, we charted our course with unparalleled determination. Strength wasn't just a physical attribute—it was a state of mind. We remained resolute, unwavering in our focus, refusing to succumb to adversity. Through perseverance and unwavering resolve, we forged ahead, steadfastly battling until the very end.

As the covering of childhood innocence gradually lifted, the stark truths of life in West Point emerged. Yet, fueled by an unwavering resolve, I resolved to transcend the confines of poverty and violence. With determination as my guide, I embarked on a journey beyond the confines of West Point, driven by a quest for knowledge and opportunity.

The path I embarked upon was widespread with challenges, each step a battle against all odds. Yet, secured by the belief that "if you make it out of West Point, you can make it anywhere," I clung to this beacon of hope even in my darkest moments. As I ventured further from home, the echoes of my past grew fainter with each stride, reminding me of my humble beginnings and the daunting journey ahead. The memories of West Point are not mere remnants of the past; they are guiding lights lighting my path into the future.

In my formative years, life in West Point began to unveil a new perspective, shedding the veil of childhood innocence. Through eyes unclouded by naivety, I witnessed the stark inequalities, pervasive crime, and entrenched poverty that overwhelmed our society. Yet, amidst these harsh realities, I also witnessed the resilient spirit of community—the shared laughter, and the unwavering unity that fortified our bonds and bonded us together as one.

My mother characterized unwavering courage and determination. Her resilience, and her unwavering commitment to safeguard her children, formed the bedrock of our survival. Alongside other courageous mothers in West Point, she waged daily wars, steadfastly surviving the unyielding storms of poverty and adversity. They nurtured and sheltered us, imparting the strength and resilience needed to navigate a world that often showed little kindness.

My mother's words echo in my mind every day: "Never forget where you came from." They serve as a constant reminder to honor my past while striving for a brighter future. It's not the circumstances of our upbringing that define us, but rather the courage and resilience we exhibit in the face of adversity.

Our modest, small homes served as our sanctuaries amidst the chaos outside. In these humble dwellings, we found comfort and safety amidst the chaos. Within those walls, we shared moments of joy and drew strength from each other's presence. United, we formed a resilient bond, a formidable force standing strong against the challenges of the outside world.

As the years passed, I became acutely aware of the world outside West Point. The tales of a better life, the stories of opportunities that lay beyond our neighborhood, started to fuel my dreams. Driven by the determination to rise above the circumstances of my birth, I began to seek knowledge and opportunities outside my community.

The journey was laden with obstacles, each step away from home feeling like a battle against overwhelming odds. Yet, the age-old wisdom echoed within me: "If you make it out of West Point, you can make it anywhere." This mantra resonated deeply, a testament to the resilience woven into my very being. So, I forged ahead, holding onto the small thread of hope, drawing strength from the echoes of my past.

With each stride away from my homeland, the echoes of my humble beginnings gradually faded into the distance. Every obstacle surmounted, every barrier shattered, served as a testament to the unbeatable spirit of West Point—a homage to the land that nurtured, molded, and equipped me for the challenges of the world.

As I embark on this new journey, a swell of pride washes over me for the myriad challenges I've conquered. I am thankful for the invaluable life lessons collected and the unwavering strength forged during my time in West Point. Regardless of where life leads me, the memories of my upbringing will forever course through my veins, shaping my character and grounding me in my roots.

Here's to West Point, to the echoes of my past that still resonate within me. Here's to the memories that molded my character, to the individuals who supported and guided me, and to the resilient spirit that fueled my journey. Here's to the trials I've faced, the victories I've earned, and the dreams I continue to pursue. Here's to Liberia, my eternal home, and to the promise of a future where every child, regardless of their origins, can aspire, persevere, and indeed, succeed anywhere. Cheers to the land of liberty, and to the boundless possibilities that lie ahead.

Looking back, I recognize that those years of hardship, of teetering on the brink of existence, of confronting adversity head-on and emerging stronger, forged the person I am today. While the streets of West Point may have been fraught with danger, they were also the breeding grounds of courage, resilience, and solidarity. They served as the crucible of life, imparting invaluable lessons of survival, tenacity, and the power of communal bonds.

For this, I owe an eternal debt of gratitude to my roots in West Point—the place that instilled in me the audacity to dream and the fortitude to pursue those dreams, undeterred by the obstacles in my path.

Today, my birthplace and childhood sanctuary, West Point, still grapples with the harsh realities of being a slum. Many, including children, endure unclean conditions, deprived of quality education.

The plague of sea erosion, a familiar adversary from my past, continues to ravage homes, leaving countless families displaced.

I hold onto hope that one day, whether through government intervention or the efforts of non-profit organizations, the residents of West Point, my fellow Liberians, will be uplifted from these dire circumstances. I pray for blessings upon my family, enabling us to contribute to the transformation of West Point into a thriving destination, preserving its rich legacy. Despite its challenges, West Point has nurtured exceptional individuals, and I am honored to count myself among them, forever indebted to my roots in this resilient community.

The resilience of West Point and its inhabitants serves as a powerful testament to the enduring strength of the human spirit in the face of adversity. It beckons us all to action, urging those who can contribute to its revitalization and progress. As we envision a brighter future for West Point, we also honor the resilience, courage, and unity it has bestowed upon us, propelling our aspirations and endeavors forward.

Here's to a future where West Point emerges as a beacon of hope, resilience, and renewal—a place that inspires generations to come with its unwavering spirit and determination.

The Township of West Point, Monrovia, Liberia, West Africa.
Alamy

THE FIRST LIBERIAN CIVIL WAR

The brilliance of the Liberian sun offered little solace to our lives, its relentless rays illuminating the worn streets of West Point, highlighting the harsh realities of our surroundings. Yet, that life now feels like a distant memory. The beginning of the Liberian Civil War's first conflict on Christmas Eve 1989 occurred when I was too young to remember anything firsthand. Instead, I collected pieces of its horrors through the narratives of my parents, elders, and the teachings of primary school. Tales of unspeakable atrocities and the devastation of lives and livelihoods flooded our collective consciousness.

Despite my tender age, there was no escaping the enduring shadow cast by the war. Its aftermath is intricately intertwined with the very essence of our existence, shaping our shared destiny in ways we could scarcely comprehend.

The onset of the second phase of the initial Liberian civil war marked a pivotal juncture in my life—it was my earliest encounter with the ravages of war. At the age of 6, I stood in the face of change, grappling with the profound implications of this shift. Amidst a brief separation between my parents, my father decided to seek refuge elsewhere. We bid farewell to the tumultuous streets of West Point, embarking on a journey towards the tranquil haven of Mamba Point—a privileged area offering the appeal of stability and normalcy amidst the chaos of conflict.

Mamba Point stood worlds apart from the rough streets of West Point. Adorned with landmarks like the United States Embassy, the European Union embassy, the pristine Graystone, and the bustling United Nations Drive, it displayed an air of affluence and sophistication. A mixture of non-governmental organizations dotted it throughout, while its diverse population—from the middle and working class to the elite—reflected a tapestry of cultures and backgrounds.

For us, the transition from West Point to Mamba Point was similar to crossing from a battlefield into an oasis of peace and prosperity. With hopes of forging a better life, we found our aspirations mirrored in the essence of this neighborhood—a manifestation of our dreams realized. Here, we could finally proclaim ourselves free from the shackles of our past.

The lingering presence of the disturbing First Liberian Civil War, spanning from December 1989 to August 1997, hung over us like a persistent shadow, refusing to dissipate. This catastrophic conflict claimed the lives of over 200,000 Liberians and displaced millions more, scattering them across neighboring nations in search of sanctuary. Among its countless tragedies, the war also subjected young men and women to exploitation, coercing them into the terrifying roles of child soldiers.

One chilling incident from this dark chapter remains engraved in my memory like an unhealed wound. Barely seven years old at the time, the atrocities of war cruelly shattered my innocence, leaving an indelible mark on my psyche.

April 6, 1996—a day etched in my memory with the intense pain of loss. The atmosphere crackled with a threatening tension as if the very air pulsed with feeling. Then, chaos erupted. In the aftermath of the calamity, three precious souls from our communal household were snatched away, leaving an irreplaceable void in our lives.

Our home was more than just a roof over our heads; it was a sanctuary of unity—a haven where individuality dissolved into a seamless tapestry of collective existence. Within its walls, love, respect, and mutual support flourished like resilient flowers amidst a harsh landscape.

Among the fallen were Papa Chea, Uncle Anastas, and Uncle Isaac—pillars of our household whose absence left a deep void. Their departure was like a black hole, engulfing the echoes of laughter, the warmth of shared meals, and the bond of familial unity that once defined us. In its wake lingered a numbness—a deep emptiness that seemed insurmountable.

I couldn't shake the thought of the memories we were robbed of—the moments we never had the chance to create together. Yet, amidst the grief, a determination stirred within us. We resolved to honor their memory and perpetuate their legacies—a testament to the enduring values of family, love, and resilience they had imparted to us. In our hearts, we carried the solemn vow to make them proud, to forge ahead with unwavering resolve, and to ensure that their spirits lived on through our actions.

Life in Mamba Point granted us access to dreams that once felt galaxies away. The school became our sanctuary, a beacon of hope in our tumultuous lives. We understood that education was our pathway to freedom. Despite its basic facilities, our school provided a refuge from the harsh realities of our world. Within its walls, we embarked on a journey of discovery, nurturing our minds with aspirations of brighter tomorrows.

The teachers emerged as our unsung heroes. Despite grappling with severe resource constraints, their commitment to service was unwavering. They believed fervently in the transformative power of education, instilling in us not just academic knowledge but also a profound sense of civic duty. One teacher, Mr. Goodridge from Elizabeth Crawford School, stood out in my memory. Despite insufficient compensation, his dedication to educating young minds like mine was evident. He selflessly invested his time and energy, often providing extra support to students, including myself, who faced academic challenges. With his guidance, I not only overcame academic hurdles but also blossomed into a leader within my class. His ethos of service continues to inspire me, shaping my outlook on life to this day.

Amidst the trials of this period, our communal household—a remnant of our West Point roots—became a sanctuary. Here, we sought solace after enduring days, finding comfort in shared stories and games. In each other's presence, we discovered peace and companionship, a relief from the burdens of life. Our backyard echoed with the sounds of joy and laughter, offering fleeting moments of bliss amidst the chaos. These cherished memories carved themselves into our hearts, a testament to the enduring bonds forged within those humble walls.

The shift from West Point to Mamba Point marked more than just a location change; it symbolized a profound change in our lives. This journey embodied our collective resilience, unshakable hope, and steadfast determination to forge a brighter path amid adversity. It served as a guiding light through our darkest hours, signaling the beginning of a new chapter in my life—a story woven with threads of despair and hope, loss, and unwavering resilience. And as each day unfolds, this narrative continues to evolve, shaped by the triumphs and trials of each new dawn.

Upon our arrival in Mamba Point, amidst the uncertainty that clouded our new beginnings, we found solace in the profound sense of community and shared purpose that mirrored the connections we had fostered back in West Point. Despite being newcomers, we were welcomed as part of the family, transcending the barriers of tribe and personality differences. This newfound unity offered not just shelter but a genuine sense of belonging, underscoring our shared resilience and capacity for adaptation.

My father, a model of diligence and culinary passion, embarked on daily trips to the waterside market to sell shoes. Evenings would see him making pepper soup and fufu, invoking the culinary traditions of Grand Bassa County, his birthplace. While his endeavors occasionally clashed with my mother's efforts to provide for the family, his frugality and entrepreneurial expertise were indispensable, ensuring we never went hungry.

In stark contrast, my mother radiated grace and selflessness. Throughout our trials, she stood as the unwavering pillar that bound our family together, her quiet strength and unwavering optimism guiding our way. Despite our struggles, her boundless generosity never wavered, fueled by a steadfast belief in divine provision. Her resilience sowed the seeds of hope and ambition within us, nurturing our dreams of a better tomorrow amidst the turmoil of our homeland.

The friendships forged in Mamba Point were truly remarkable. Each family, with its unique cultural heritage and customs, contributed to the vibrant fabric of our communal existence, fostering a deep sense of shared identity. This transformation marked a departure from our past but affirmed our innate capacity to adapt and flourish, even in the face of adversity.

Despite the appearance of normalcy that life in Mamba Point provided, the possibility of war lingered on. Reports of ongoing conflict, of loved ones lost, and dreams shattered by violence were a grim reality. We dwelled in the shadow of war, our moments of relief tainted by reminders of our chaotic homeland. Yet, we refused to succumb to despair. We recognized that our journey was far from over. The tragedies of our past served as poignant reminders of life's fragility, yet they also fueled our resolve, propelling us forward with unwavering determination.

Mamba Point, Monrovia, Liberia, West Africa.
Getty Images

THE LOSSES AND MIRACLES

In a single minute, life's path can drastically shift, turning from the ordinary to the extraordinary, from the normal to the miraculous. A mere sixty seconds can set between the comforting sizzle of cooking and the crashing roar of destruction. This harsh truth was utterly evident on a fateful day etched into our collective consciousness. A threatening rocket, an unwelcome guest, pierced the sanctity of our shared home, forever altering the landscape where we once gathered for daily meals, and tragically claimed three beloved lives.

In my mother's retelling, she was touched by a divine miracle. Mere moments before the catastrophic explosion, she stood at what would soon become the epicenter, engaged in the simple act of preparing our meal. A signaling call from inside our home lured her away, creating a life-saving distance between her and threatening disaster. This seemingly ordinary departure became her salvation from the approaching tragedy. In the aftermath, as dust settled and debris scattered the scene, she felt only the tremors of the aftermath, a powdery residue creeping in through the window. It was nothing short of a miracle that she emerged to share the traumatic tale.

The sudden departure of Papa Chea, Uncle Anastas, and Uncle Isaac left a profound void in our lives. Their absence echoed like an open wound, vibrating with relentless pain. The spaces they once filled with laughter and wisdom now stood silent, a stark reminder of their absence. Their loss weighed heavily on us, especially for those they left behind to grapple with grief. Their absence lingered like an unseen presence, casting a shadow over every meal and conversation. The memories of their laughter and companionship served as poignant reminders of the brutal toll of war.

The tragedy also struck our biological family, claiming the life of my Uncle Joseph, fondly called JJ. Uncle JJ was my look-alike, a reflection of myself in many ways. My mother often remarked on our uncanny resemblance, from our complexion to our sense of humor and behavior. His absence left a profound void within our family, a haunting absence that threatened to unravel the fabric of our shared identity.

The circumstances surrounding Uncle JJ's death remained shrouded in mystery, a constant source of anguish for our family. Unlike the others, his body was never recovered, denying us the closure of a proper farewell. The unanswered questions surrounding his fate cast a shadow over our lives, serving as a poignant reminder of the turmoil and uncertainty caused by war. Each day, the absence of answers deepened our sense of loss, transforming Uncle JJ's memory into a mystery covered in perpetual sorrow.

The divine intervention that spared my mother's life that fateful day became a pillar of our faith. Her survival stood as a miraculous testament to our resilience in the face of adversity. Whenever the shadows of despair loomed large, we found solace in her survival, a tangible reminder of the blessings bestowed upon us. We remained grateful, recognizing her survival as nothing short of a divine miracle.

We were resilient. Each member of our family—my mother, my siblings, and the remaining members of our shared household—drew strength from within to overcome our circumstances. We embraced the vision of a brighter tomorrow, the longing for peace, and the aspiration for a better future. Our unity strengthened; our determination unwavering. Despite the chaos, we pressed on, fueled by courage and sustained by hope.

Life is fleeting and fragile, yet remarkably resilient—a flame that persists against all odds. My passage from West Point to Mamba Point, from hardship to a semblance of stability, epitomizes this paradox. It is a narrative of endurance, of defiance in the face of adversity, of hope's enduring power, and the unbreakable spirit of humanity.

Reflecting on my journey, I see a tapestry rich with threads of love and loss, hope and despair, resilience and surrender. Each thread represents a chapter of my life, and each knot signifies a pivotal moment that has sculpted me into the person I am today.

As I stand at this juncture, the story of my life unfolds with countless threads yet to be woven and knots yet to be tied. Gratitude fills my heart for the journey, the lessons, the love, and even the loss. It is these experiences that have molded me, crafted me, and defined the person I am today.

THE ROCK AND THE RESILIENCE

The news of Uncle Joseph's death shattered us, leaving a void that seemed impossible to fill. My mother, devastated by the loss, embarked on a desperate quest for answers, determined to uncover the truth behind her brother's untimely death.

She wandered through the streets of West Point, questioning anyone who might know his whereabouts. Yet, her efforts yielded no results. The search was a painful reminder of the harsh realities she wished to escape. Uncle JJ's absence left a deep void that seemed insurmountable. Though I have only faint memories of him from my childhood, the tales of his compassion, benevolence, and affection served as emotional reminders of his character.

His passing had a profound impact on my grandmother, for Uncle JJ was not only her firstborn but also the foundation of her family's lineage. The anguish she endured was incomprehensible to me, weighing heavily on her heart like a burden too immense to bear. His absence cast a profound silence over her life, a void that seemed impossible to fill. The unresolved questions surrounding his death and the ensuing grief left a lasting mark on our family, a wound that time has yet to fully mend.

The losses extended beyond Uncle JJ alone. Papa Chea, Uncle Anastas, and Uncle Isaac were pillars in our community, and their absence was a profound disruption that resounded through the core of our existence. They weren't just individuals; they were integral to our shared identity, and their lives connected with ours in countless ways. Each loss felt like a monumental event, gradually reshaping the fabric of the life we once knew.

Papa Chea held a special place in our lives, particularly in mine. A close friend of my father, their connection began during one of their regular evening gatherings. Papa Chea generously offered my father a room in his house, which soon became our family's sanctuary within the shared household. This gesture symbolized their profound bond and unwavering friendship. His wife, Ma Elizabeth, fondly called Ma Kortie, embodied grace. Her spirit radiated like the morning sun, and her resilience and fortitude were truly remarkable.

Uncle Anastas was another cherished soul in our community. A pastor by calling, he possessed a profound faith, his words carrying a weight that left a lasting impact. His wife, Mrs. Roberta, affectionately known as Auntie, radiated the same warmth and love. Their relationship was a beautiful tapestry woven with threads of mutual respect and unwavering devotion, a testament to the enduring bonds that bound us together.

Uncle Isaac's tale, as shared by his elder brother, Uncle William, adds another layer to our collective memories. Isaac wasn't merely intelligent and kind; he was a source of support and happiness within our home, always ready to assist his older brother with chores. His love for football ran deep, often leading him to prioritize the game over his studies. Affectionately nicknamed "Older Time" by his peers, Isaac's talent on the field was undeniable, culminating in a selection for the junior Lonestar team, a significant step toward his dream of representing the national team.

Tragically, Isaac's life was abruptly ended in a horrific event—a rocket strike that shattered the calm near our home, claiming not only Isaac but also Uncle Chea and Anastas. The memory of that chaos remains vivid; I can still feel the disorienting shock that gripped me when I returned to find Isaac lying in the grass, blood seeping from his wounds. As I knelt beside him, his blood staining my face, he pleaded with a heartbreaking urgency, 'Take me to the clinic, brother.' Despite our desperate efforts, we couldn't save him. Recalling that moment reopens old wounds, resurrecting the raw anguish of his untimely departure."

Our lives were infused with a resilient spirit despite the catastrophe. Our loved ones' passing kindled a flame inside of us and served as a lighthouse in the shadows. This fortitude and unwavering spirit served as our invisible armor and shield from the unrelenting assault of life's hardships. This resiliency strengthened our spirits, helped us get through the rough seas of bereavement, and opened the door to a bright and promising future.

During this period of profound sorrow, ordinary tasks became our lifelines. The simple acts of waking up, preparing meals, and caring for each other became acts of defiance against the overwhelming pain we endured. Each day felt like a battle, a relentless struggle against the hardships that besieged us. Yet, with time, we began to recognize the resilience blooming within us, nurtured by our trials and tribulations.

My mother, in particular, exhibited remarkable strength in coping with the loss of her beloved brother and the profound void it left behind. Despite the weight of her grief, she remained steadfast and dignified. Each day, she faced adversity with unwavering determination, as though every step she took was a tribute to her love for Uncle JJ and her commitment to preserving his memory. She often regaled us with stories of him, choosing to focus not on the sorrow of his premature departure, but rather on the richness of his vibrant personality. Through these anecdotes, I came to know a man who found joy in life's simplest pleasures, whose heart overflowed with generosity, and whose laughter was infectious. In Uncle JJ, I discovered an indomitable spirit, a testament to the resilience of the human soul.

Ma Kortie, with her unwavering strength and deep faith, became the cornerstone of our household, her presence a steadfast reminder that hope endures even in the darkest of times. Auntie Robertha, carrying forward Uncle Anastas's legacy, emerged as a beacon of hope, guiding us through our mourning with unwavering faith.

With each passing day, our resilience grew stronger. We discovered the ability to find joy amidst sorrow, to treasure every moment, and to honor the lives of our departed loved ones not with tears, but with love and celebration. Despite the profoundness of our grief, we discovered a strength and spirit that defied all odds—a testament to the enduring power of love and resilience.

Uncle William's presence during Uncle Isaac's final moments, witnessing the heart-wrenching loss firsthand, added a profound depth to our collective sorrow. The memory of Isaac's last words, 'Take me to the clinic, brother,' and the haunting imagery of his final moments remain etched in our hearts, poignant reminders of life's fragility. Yet, through Uncle William's eyes, we also glimpse the unwavering strength of family bonds, a testament to the enduring love that sustains us through even the darkest of times.

As I record these memories, the ache of losing cherished ones still resides within my heart, yet so does the strength we unearthed and the enduring power of love. Despite grappling with loss and grief, we uncovered an extraordinary human resilience and an unbeatable spirit. We came to understand that even in the wake of profound loss, life persists, hope prevails, and love remains steadfast. Through the trials of our past, we forged a path toward a future teeming with promise—a testament to the enduring resilience of the human spirit. The memories of our departed loved ones no longer merely evoke the pain of a former era; they stand as symbols of our resilience, fortitude, and unwavering optimism for tomorrow. In this optimism, we discover solace—a tribute to those we've lost and a celebration of the miracle of life.

This spot at our Mamba Point home was where my mother escaped a rocket by a single minute as she went inside our room to get cooking oil.

Courtesy of my younger sister, Siah.

2

Under the Shadow of War

"OUT OF SUFFERING HAVE EMERGED THE STRONGEST SOULS; THE MOST MASSIVE CHARACTERS ARE SEARED WITH SCARS." – KHALIL GIBRAN

The outbreak of war in Liberia was sudden, turning an ordinary day into a whirlwind of chaos, where the peace of daily life swiftly gave way to the discordant symphony of conflict. In an instant, the innocence of childhood was shattered by fear, as the familiar sounds of play were drowned out by the relentless barrage of gunfire and the piercing wails of sirens. This chapter delves into one of the most turbulent periods of my life—the continuation of the first Liberian Civil War—a time marked by profound disruption and a shift in my perception of existence.

The war irrevocably altered our lives, resulting in the loss of loved ones, the devastation of homes, and the abrupt end of our childhood. These events left enduring scars on our minds and hearts. Yet, amid the narratives of loss, tales of courage, resilience, and survival emerged. Amidst the chaos, people banded together, offering support and protection, often at great personal peril. In the darkest of times, they clung to their humanity. These unsung heroes, though their names may never adorn any monument, kindled hope with their actions.

This chapter is more than just a retelling of the darkness brought by war; it's also a celebration of the resilience that blossomed in its wake, the invaluable lessons learned, and the profound strength discovered amidst adversity. As we journey forward, let's cling to the belief that every storm unveils a rainbow, and every night announces the dawn of a new day.

Our home lovingly referred to as 'The Rock,' stood as a symbol of our community's unwavering spirit. Despite its rugged and imposing exterior, it served as fertile ground for nurturing a resilient and close-knit family. These dwellings, scattered across the landscape, were more than mere shelters; they embodied our collective determination to overcome adversity. Nestled among the towering rocks, they bore witness to the perseverance, ingenuity, and adaptability of those who called this challenging terrain their home.

Partially constructed from the very stones that defined the area, our home served as the heartbeat of our community—a testament to endurance and resolve. Its sturdy walls echoed the resilience of its inhabitants, symbolizing our unity and collective determination.

Growing up among these imposing natural structures was an adventure in itself, teaching us to navigate their sharp edges with caution and embrace the challenges they posed. Our childhood games, inspired by the rugged terrain, served as tests of our resilience and nurtured our spirits.

I was affectionately dubbed 'Ericboy,' or simply 'Oldboy' by my younger sister Siah, who struggled to pronounce my name. This nickname echoed my role within our household, where I took charge of running errands and contributing to our daily necessities. Rather than viewing these tasks as burdensome, I saw them as integral to the smooth functioning of our home, highlighting our shared responsibilities and unity.

One vivid memory etched in my mind is the task of fetching water from the well, which resulted in a severe injury when I tripped and fell on a sharp rock. The accident, requiring 12 stitches above my eyebrows, left a permanent scar—a stark reminder of the risks and responsibilities associated with our unique living situation.

Our household was a lively microcosm, a community within a community, where every member played a vital role. Together, we forged a harmonious and functional living space—a symphony of life in which each person contributed to the collective melody.

The Rock, with its stark beauty and challenging conditions, was not just a backdrop but an active participant in our daily lives. Without the luxury of modern conveniences like washing machines or dryers, we relied on these rugged rocks to dry our clothes in the sun. This experience instilled in us the values of hard work, unity, and the beauty found in simplicity. Despite its cold and hard exterior, we found warmth in each other's company, joy in our shared experiences, and strength in our collective resilience.

As I reflect on my past, I realize the profound and lasting impact The Rock has had on me. It served as a silent mentor, imparting lessons in resilience, adaptability, and the importance of unity. The echoes of laughter and shared moments still echo within me, guiding my path forward. Despite its imposing appearance, The Rock will always be a part of me—a reminder of my roots and the indomitable strength of the human spirit.

REFUGE AND SURVIVAL

Our home on The Rock transcended mere shelter; it was a bustling community of interconnected relationships—a tapestry woven from diverse experiences and cherished memories, bound together by a sense of togetherness, resilience, and love. It served as our sanctuary, a place where we could gather in moments of both joy and sorrow. We were more than just individuals; we were family, united by an unbreakable bond and a shared sense of belonging to something greater than ourselves.

The aroma of the various meals prepared by our mothers permeated the air, enticing us all to indulge in the delectable spread. Each dish bore the unmistakable imprint of love and dedication. In our youth, we circled the table like planetary bodies orbiting a radiant sun, eager to sample every culinary creation. The act of sharing meals transcended mere routine; it constituted a cherished tradition that fostered intimacy among our chosen family, fortifying the ties that bound us together.

The laughter and lively chat that vibrated throughout our home were the sweet symphonies of our shared existence. Amidst the hustle and bustle of daily life, amidst the clatter of pots and pans in the kitchen, we found a unique tone, a harmony that infused our dwelling with the essence of belonging. In our childhood, we lie down on mats and mattresses alongside our parents, or gathered in the living room to sleep, each taking our own space in the cozy confines, for our parents' rooms were too cramped to accommodate us all. These moments of togetherness—gathered around the dinner table, swapping stories and laughter—imprinted lasting memories upon my heart.

As I matured, my perspective broadened, casting a wider gaze upon the landscape of my homeland, Liberia. Here, amidst the fertile beauty, lay the stark reminders of its turbulent history, engraved in the scars of conflict that stained its soil. The worrying beat of war drums echoed threateningly, a constant reminder even within the relative sanctuary of The Rock.

When violence erupted once more in September 1996, we were forced into flight, seeking sanctuary from the chaos that engulfed our surroundings. Our journey back to West Point, my birthplace, represented our collective resilience. With each stride, we moved not only toward a physical destination but toward the promise of security, solace, and communal survival.

Our arrival in West Point wasn't merely a return to familiar streets; it was a tender reunion, a rekindling of unity, solidarity, and mutual reliance. In this moment, we found ourselves bound together once more by the unbreakable threads of shared experience and communal strength.

As I matured amidst the trials of a society in turmoil, I found myself akin to a sponge, eagerly soaking up the myriad experiences, stories, and wisdom that surrounded me. My grandparents exemplified resilience in the face of adversity, my parents imparted lessons of adaptability, and my surrogate siblings brightened the strength born of unity. Each individual I encountered became a vital chapter in the narrative of my life, offering invaluable insights, shaping my worldview, and sculpting my character with their unique contributions.

When recalling my past, my thoughts inevitably gravitate towards The Rock, the backdrop against which pivotal chapters of my life unfolded. It stood as a paradoxical sanctuary—a formidable stronghold that cradled within its walls the fragile beauty of familial bonds, unity, and unwavering resilience. It was within those hallowed confines that I collected the profound lesson that even amidst life's harshest trials, hope can flourish, love can persevere, and joy can be unearthed.

The Rock transcended its physicality; it left an indelible mark upon the my existence, serving as an emotional symbol of our collective fortitude, tenacity, and enduring optimism in the face of adversity.

Today, I stand tall, not despite the trials I've weathered, but because of the fortitude and solidarity instilled in me by my family. The vibrant tapestry of life upon The Rock was a symphony of laughter shared, jests exchanged, and melodies sung from the depths of our souls. Each day was punctuated by the rhythmic pulse of existence, resonating with the harmonious chords of unity. The carefree laughter of children at play, the melodious lilt of my mother's storytelling, the hushed confidences exchanged between siblings, and the sage counsel of our elders—all intertwined to form the rich chorus of our collective journey.

In the world of childhood, joy frequently springs from the most unexpected sources. Within the rugged landscape of our playground, a modest patch of sand became an unexpected oasis, a haven of delight amid the harsh terrain. Here, in this humble sanctuary, we crafted our own realm of imagination. Our creativity transformed milk containers and old batteries into makeshift cars. When we weren't in school, we played marbles in the sand and on the streets. Despite the looming shadow of war, we reveled in the simple joys of camaraderie and creativity.

Upon our homecoming to West Point, we sought solace in the comforting embrace of the familiar. Though our resources were small, we united in resourcefulness, making the most of what little we possessed, thereby reaffirming our collective strength and resilience. Food like fufu and cabbage surpassed simple provisions; it emerged as a potent symbol of our shared endurance, a tangible reminder of our capacity to adapt and thrive in the most trying of circumstances. With each meal shared, we celebrated not only our survival but also the unbreakable bond that bound us together as a community.

The lessons learned from my time on The Rock have fortified me with the resilience and courage necessary to navigate life's most rocky paths. The core values instilled within me during those formative years have proven invaluable, empowering me to confront any obstacle with unwavering determination.

The profound sense of community and interconnectedness cultivated within The Rock's embrace has not only enriched my life but has also shaped me into a more compassionate and empathetic individual. I am eternally grateful for the memories and experiences bestowed upon me, for they serve as constant reminders of the strength found in unity and the enduring power of human connection.

"The Rock", our shared household on Mamba Point, Monrovia, Liberia, West Africa.
Courtesy of my younger sister, Siah.

CHILDHOOD REBELLIOUSNESS

Following the 1997 elections, Liberia experienced a semblance of peace, though simmering tensions persisted. Despite the appearance of stability, discontent brewed among certain leaders, particularly regarding Charles Taylor's election. It was within this fragile peace that my adolescence unfolded—a time characterized by exploration, peer influence, and occasional defiance.

In my case, this portrayal couldn't be more appropriate. My inner turmoil mirrored a stormy sea crying for liberation. The familiar streets of Mamba Point, once echoing with my carefree laughter and youthful adventures, became the arena for my growing defiance. The days of my childhood, spent as a humble errand boy running among the rocks and enjoying the familial warmth, now felt like distant echoes. Caught in the chaotic currents of rebellion, I found myself torn between the innocence of my past and the fearless defiance shaping my present identity.

This transformation within me didn't occur suddenly; rather, it unfolded gradually, driven by the lasting scars of the civil war and fueled by my unyielding adolescent defiance. Continuously pushing boundaries, I tested the limits of the bonds connecting me to the authority figures in my life. My actions became a reflection of my inner turmoil, a tangible expression of the chaos brewing within.

Nights became hollow stretches, my room was left cold and barren, devoid of my presence. Each morning, my parents faced the stark emptiness of my absence, a void deepening with each passing day. Where laughter and joy once echoed, now lingered a haunting silence, a poignant testament to the growing break between us. The child they once cradled in their arms, whose laughter once filled our home, now seemed a distant memory, obscured behind the façade of rebellion.

One fateful day, my defiance escalated beyond acceptable bounds. Following a confrontation with my mother that resulted in punishment, I decided to flee. I sought refuge at a friend's house, located a mile from our school, in a desperate attempt to escape consequences, authority, and guilt. For a week, I lived secretly under the radar, shielded from detection by the school authorities, thanks to the cover my friend provided.

Meanwhile, my parents were consumed by worry and helplessness. Their minds raced with thoughts of my whereabouts, enveloped in a shroud of uncertainty. Time, once a constant companion, now weighed heavily upon them, each passing second a painful reminder of my absence. Every ounce of their being was devoted to locating me, their hearts heavy with longing and concern.

One day, the unbearable tension of my absence was shattered by an unexpected reunion. A friend from our shared community spotted me near my hiding place and promptly informed my parents, igniting a spark of hope within them. With determined resolve, they embarked on the mission to find their estranged son. I vividly recall that Saturday morning—the soft glow of dawn casting a gentle light upon my parents' faces, a blend of relief, worry, and hope etched across their features against the tranquil backdrop of our neighborhood. My father's older sister stood by their side, her reassuring presence lending a sense of calm to the fraught situation. Initially, I harbored a desire to flee and evade their potential anger, but my aunt's gentle reassurance ultimately persuaded me to return to the comforting embrace of home.

Reflecting on the past, I can only begin to grasp the depth of pain and helplessness my parents endured during my absence. It required immense strength for them to remain resolute amidst uncertainty. My return signaled the end of this tumultuous chapter, and enrolling in a mission boarding school offered me a chance for a fresh start. Determined to amend my ways, I embraced the opportunity for redemption.

The structured and tranquil environment of the mission boarding school stood in stark contrast to the tumultuous streets I once roamed. Surrounded by discipline and order, I found myself on a transformative journey, distancing myself from the recklessness of my past and forging a new path forward.

The school transcended mere institutional walls; it became a sanctuary, a refuge that provided much-needed guidance to my tumultuous adolescent journey. With each class, sermon, and discipline enforced, it felt as though my once-chaotic spirit was undergoing a profound transformation, navigating me toward the shores of maturity.

Life within the boarding school was characterized by a strict regimen of discipline, punctuated by our daily rituals, from the pre-dawn prayers to the evening church service. The serene atmosphere of the school stood in stark contrast to the turmoil still pervasive in the outside world, haunted by the aftermath of the civil war. In essence, the mission boarding school served as a peaceful oasis amidst the turbulent waters of the surrounding chaos.

The school's rigorous schedule instilled in me the virtues of discipline and punctuality, principles that I embraced as I matured. Within the confines of this remarkable institution, I discovered the significance of education, the thrill of acquiring knowledge, and a passion for reading and expanding my vocabulary. Driven by a fervent desire to learn, I sought solace and stimulation in the pages of newspapers, magazines, and dictionaries. This diverse reading material fueled my curiosity and nurtured my intellectual growth.

I found myself delving into any book I came across, captivated by the enchantment of words. I developed a habit of jotting down unfamiliar words and looking them up in the dictionary to enhance my vocabulary. Through the pages of those books and newspapers,

I embarked on journeys far removed from the rocky landscapes and war-torn streets of my childhood, finding inspiration and solace in realms of knowledge and wisdom beyond my wildest dreams.

As my rebellious spirit gradually waned, I forged meaningful connections with both my peers and teachers. Respect and admiration replaced my previous defiance. The teachers, with their patient and empathetic demeanor, became instrumental in my transformation, gently guiding me through the complexities of adolescence with wisdom and understanding.

Life within the mission boarding school was not solely defined by discipline and academia; it also brimmed with moments of joy and camaraderie. The dormitory, our haven during leisure hours, buzzed with laughter, gossip, and playful behaviors. It was within these walls that friendships blossomed, rivalries flourished, and cherished memories were etched into the fabric of our lives, destined to endure the test of time.

In the quiet of the night, we would gather, huddled close, exchanging tales of our homes and families. These intimate conversations infused warmth into our otherwise routine existence, weaving vibrant threads into the fabric of our shared experiences. Despite hailing from diverse backgrounds, we formed a cohesive unit, a motley crew of boys with distinct narratives, yet united by common dreams and aspirations.

Looking back, I recognize that my tenure at the mission boarding school transcended mere academics and discipline; it was a profound voyage of self-discovery and personal evolution. Amidst those transformative years, I gleaned invaluable lessons in responsibility, resilience, and respect for others. The myriad experiences within those hallowed walls not only shaped my worldview but also furnished me with a compass for navigating life's complexities. Equipped with newfound wisdom and life skills, I embarked on the journey ahead, fortified by the indelible imprint of my time at the school.

Looking back, I realize that my adolescent rebellion was not merely a phase of disobedience; it was a poignant expression of my inner turmoil, a quest for self-awareness amidst the tumultuous currents of life. It was a desperate plea for guidance amid the chaos that engulfed me. Ultimately, it was my time at the mission boarding school that served as my guiding light, redirecting me from the path of recklessness toward a journey of self-discovery and maturity.

THE QUEST TO SAVE A TROUBLED CHILD

As the departure date for the mission drew near, anxiety and uncertainty weighed heavily on my mind. My meager belongings, along with some food and snacks, were hastily packed into a "Ghana Must Go" bag. Together with my parents, we embarked on a journey along the rugged Liberian roads aboard a public bus. Despite attempts to hum a tune, a sense of melancholy pervaded my thoughts as we made our way toward what would soon become my new home, leaving behind my younger sisters, Queen and Siah, and the rest of our shared household members on Mamba Point. Though tinged with sadness, the journey was deemed necessary for my future.

The mission was nestled in the heart of Gardnersville Township, specifically within the Chicken Soup Factory community of the Greater Monrovia District, Liberia. Its peculiar name derived from a defunct factory that once manufactured Maggi chicken bouillon cubes nearby. Situated in this somewhat secluded area, it provided a welcome respite from the chaotic hustle and bustle of Monrovia. Spanning across acres of land, its expansive campus served as an oasis of serenity amidst the tumultuous surroundings.

The main building, a weathered single-story structure housing multiple units, boasted brick walls adorned with the layer of time, while iron-barred windows stood as a testament to the institution's strict discipline. A vast playground stretched out in front of it, flanked by dormitories, a dining hall, and a church, completing the ensemble of facilities.

The mission was established with the noble purpose of providing a home for children who had been orphaned by the ravages of war or were unable to be cared for by their families. Some, like myself, were sent there due to our rebellious tendencies. Welcoming us with open arms were the founders and caretakers of the mission, Mr. and

Mrs. Morrison, whose kind smiles and comforting words immediately eased the apprehension of my parents. Their presence exuded an aura of unwavering faith and determination, instilling a sense of reassurance in all who crossed their path.

Mrs. Morrison, a gentle middle-aged woman, possessed a warm smile that almost concealed the underlying strength in her eyes. Meanwhile, Mr. Morrison, a tall and sturdy figure, had a stern countenance softened by the kindness reflected in his gaze. Together, they exemplified a harmonious unity, embodying the delicate balance between discipline and compassion, and between enforcing rules and fostering understanding that they aimed to instill in their us.

Once enrolled, my life underwent a complete turnaround. The days were meticulously structured, governed by a stringent routine that allowed little leeway for misbehavior. From morning church services to classroom sessions, from manual labor to retreating to our dormitories at sunset, every moment was meticulously scheduled. The rules were explicit, and any deviation was swiftly met with appropriate consequences—a stark departure from the impulsive freedom I had grown accustomed to. Though the transition was drastic and occasionally overwhelming, it proved to be precisely what I needed—a jarring awakening to veer me away from my rebellious path.

In this disciplined environment, my rebellious tendencies were met with firm but fair discipline. At times, the urge to defy authority was strong, yet the Morrison's consistent approach and the silent support of my peers kept me grounded. Over time, I transformed. The urge to rebel gradually waned, replaced by a newfound appreciation for rules and structure. Alongside this, a sense of responsibility began to take root within me.

The transition was far from smooth. Each day felt like an uphill battle, a relentless struggle against my inner turmoil. Yet, as time progressed, I gradually acclimated to this unfamiliar landscape. The once-oppressive discipline evolved from a weighty burden into a guiding beacon. While I was still far from flawless, noticeable improvements began to emerge, evident to those in my midst.

While the structured routine played a significant role, it was the sense of camaraderie among us boarders that truly catalyzed my transformation. Our shared experiences, collective struggles, and shared victories fostered a bond that transcended mere friendship—we were a family, united not by blood but by shared adversity and a common pursuit of personal growth. Within this unique familial bond, I discovered a sense of belonging that helped me navigate the complexities of adolescence.

Moreover, this transition wasn't solely about discipline and personal transformation; it was also about uncovering my potential. The mission provided me with opportunities that expanded my horizons. Through reading and vocabulary exercises, I gained insight into the world beyond my immediate surroundings. What initially seemed daunting soon became tools that empowered me to confront life's challenges, paving the way for a future that once felt out of reach.

Throughout this difficult journey, my parents remained steadfast in their belief in me. Their regular visits served as tangible evidence of their unwavering support, their eyes glowing with pride at my ongoing transformation, their arms always open for a reassuring embrace. Though they seldom vocalized their sentiments, their actions spoke volumes. With each passing day, as I evolved and matured, they stood by my side, silent witnesses to my growth, cherishing every moment of my journey toward becoming the person I was meant to be.

Looking back, I realize that the mission was more than just a place of rehabilitation—it was a crucible of transformation. Within its walls, I shed the cloak of juvenile defiance and emerged with the wings of maturity and discipline. It was a journey defined by trials and triumphs, by lessons learned and futures shaped. Amidst the structured routines, shared meals, classroom lessons, and deepening friendships, I discovered my true self. Here, Ericboy, the rebellious adolescent, evolved into a young man brimming with dreams and potential. It was within these hallowed halls that I found my footing, poised to soar and explore the vast horizons that lay ahead. For this, I am eternally grateful to my parents, to the Morrison's, and to the mission that offered me a lifeline when I was on the face of losing myself.

My arrival at the mission was both frightening and exciting. The first day was a whirlwind of introductions and a deluge of instructions to absorb. The surroundings were a stark departure from the sandy beaches of West Point and the rocky terrain of Mamba Point. Instead, I was greeted by lush green fields, a central building housing classrooms and dormitories, and a chapel standing proudly at the heart of the campus—a poignant symbol of the mission's faith-based ethos.

Every student at the mission bore a unique narrative, a personal odyssey that had brought them to this sanctuary. Some were orphaned by the brutal toll of the civil war, their lives shattered and reshaped by its unforgiving grip. Others, like myself, hailed from families drawn to the mission's promise of renewal and redemption. We formed a mosaic of humanity, a kaleidoscope of diverse backgrounds, experiences, and circumstances, united by the common thread of seeking transformation within these walls.

The initial weeks at the mission were a tumultuous ride of emotions. Amidst feelings of homesickness, anxiety, and occasional resentment towards my parents for their decision, I also encountered acts of kindness, forged friendships, and embraced the discipline instilled within the structured environment. Each day unfolded with a predictable rhythm: morning and evening prayer sessions, communal meals shared in the dining hall, equitable distribution of chores, and an engaging academic schedule that kept us mentally stimulated and focused.

Within the mission's confines, discipline wasn't merely a tool for correction, but a means of nurturing responsibility and self-awareness. Every directive and task carried with it a deeper lesson, not just in obedience and respect, but also in resilience, empathy, and compassion. The leaders of the mission, including the couple and their dedicated staff, embodied these values through their actions, serving as living examples of the virtues they aimed to instill in us. Their unwavering commitment made us recognize that we were part of a collective endeavor, fostering a sense of belonging and purpose larger than ourselves.

As time passed, the mission gradually molded me, shifting my identity far from the rebellious teenager I once embodied. I started grasping the significance of respect, discipline, and perseverance. Amidst the challenges of mission life, I gleaned insight into the rationale behind my parents' challenging choice. Their love and aspirations for my future resonated through the mission's principles and lessons. Their unwavering belief in me, mirrored in the mission's faith-based teachings, became my beacon, directing me towards a journey of self-improvement and change.

Reflecting on the past, I come to understand that the mission transcended mere education and discipline. It served as a refuge, a haven offering me belonging, purpose, and direction. Within its walls, I unearthed my capabilities and cultivated a profound respect for others, and above all, for myself. It became the crucible in which my resilience was forged, where I honed my capacity to surmount obstacles, and where I nurtured an aspiration to evolve into a superior iteration of myself.

Reflecting on the transformative odyssey that commenced at The Rock and continued through the mission, I realize that the path I traversed, replete with rugged terrain and arduous ascents, symbolized more than just rebellion, discipline, and metamorphosis. It epitomized the resilience inherent in the human spirit, showcasing our capacity to endure and transcend. It underscored the profound influence of faith, love, and hope in shaping our destinies. This journey bestowed upon me invaluable wisdom molded my principles and steered me toward the individual I am today. For this, I am forever indebted to The Rock, the mission, and above all, to my parents, whose unwavering belief in me and boundless affection guided me along this path of evolution and self-discovery.

THE MISSION - DISCIPLINE AND HARDSHIPS

Each dawn, the dormitories were lit up by early morning sunlight, awakening us from sleep with unyielding insistence. There was no luxury of lingering in bed; we were propelled into action. At the mission, bathing became a communal affair, resembling soldiers preparing for battle, with boys and girls directed to separate bathrooms. A large pot, scented with the smell of burning wood, served as our makeshift water heater. However, with so many of us needing to bathe, the water often grew cold before everyone's turn. At times, we had to shower with cold water, especially when the older folks failed to wake up early to heat it. This abrupt chill, much like an alarm clock, starkly reminded us of the harsh realities within the mission's confines.

Each day adhered to a stringent routine of morning prayer, followed by chores, school, more chores, evening prayers, meals, and finally, bedtime. This monotonous cycle, though rigid and boring, transcended mere routine over time. It served as a crucible, molding and fortifying our characters, even effecting a transformation in those once prone to rebellion, instilling discipline where there was defiance. Within the sanctuary of the chapel, amidst the rigidity of the mission's regulations, we found solace. Day after day, we were enveloped by the harmonies of hymns, the prayers, and the solace of faith. I found myself captivated by the resonant tones of the drum, the fervent supplications, and the narratives of hope and redemption that permeated the space. Faith emerged as my steadfast anchor, offering solace amidst the unforgiving strictures of life within the mission's confines.

As for whether this rigorous discipline was truly transformative, I cannot definitively say. Despite the stringent measures imposed upon me, my inherent free spirit remained unyielding, my rebellious nature unbroken. Even upon departing from the mission's confines, I remained the restless young man who often kept his mother awake with worry. My journey was far from its conclusion; the mission had merely laid the groundwork for what was to come.

I remember my time at the mission like it was yesterday. The day I left is crystal clear in my mind. The journey from my home in Monrovia to the mission felt like it took forever. It was only thirty miles, but it seemed like a huge gap between where I came from and where I was going. Every mile made me feel farther from home and closer to the unknown.

Arriving at the mission felt like stepping into a whole new world. At the heart of it all was Mrs. Morrison, the headmistress, who would become a crucial figure during my time there. She was a woman of grace, kindness, and authority, a steady presence amid the challenges of mission life. But alongside her gentleness was a firm commitment to discipline, enforced rigorously by her husband, the mission's co-founder. The first time I faced his disciplinary measures, it felt like a shock of cold water, a sudden realization of the strictness that defined life at the mission.

As time passed, the mission started to feel less unfamiliar and more like a place I belonged to. My relationships with my peers grew into deep friendships. The differences that once separated us, like where we came from or our backgrounds, didn't seem to matter as much anymore. We weren't just classmates or roommates; we were like family.

One of the strongest connections I formed was with Junior, a fellow companion in our journey at the mission. We leaned on each other for support as we navigated the trials the mission threw our way. Our bond grew through shared tales, laughter, and the meals our parents sent us. I remember times when we would enjoy 'Garri'—a staple made from cassava root—mixed with sugar and peanuts from the same plate, along with other treats our parents provided. Our friendship felt unbreakable, so when Junior passed away, it felt like a piece of me went with him.

Sadly, Junior was taken from us by illness far too soon. The night he lost his battle remains vivid in my memory—the eerie silence, his vacant bed, and his laughter echoing as a bittersweet memory. His departure left a void in my heart, profoundly altering my perspective on life and death, the value of friendship, and the agony of loss. It was a harsh lesson, but one that molded me deeply.

Despite the sorrow of loss and the strict rules, the mission became my sanctuary, molding and readying me for the challenges beyond its walls. The friendships I forged, the wisdom I gained, and the principles I absorbed in that modest environment played a pivotal role in shaping who I am. I look back with gratitude for the journey that brought me to the mission and the profound changes it sparked within me.

At the mission, everyone, regardless of age, pitched in by participating in communal chores. We organized into teams to venture into the bush to gather firewood, often trekking miles and crossing rivers, sometimes more than one. Occasionally, we embarked on lengthy journeys to gather chicken greens, a special feed for the pigs raised by the mission's founders. Our efforts were vital for the welfare of these animals, making it feel like a true test of our resilience. Additionally, we engaged in farming under the guidance of the older members of the mission.

I vividly recall my first experience gathering firewood. Being new and inexperienced, the meager bundle I managed to collect earned me laughter and the nickname "Pema" from the other children, who teased me for what they perceived as laziness. The nickname stemmed from an incident where I was beaten with a stick—ironically, one that we had gathered from the forest for firewood—because I failed to complete my chores. My usual partner's absence that day left me struggling alone. Struggling to pronounce Mr.

Morrison's name, the mission's founder, I mistakeably said "Pema" during the reprimand. That first wood-gathering excursion proved particularly daunting for me; I struggled to carry my load until one of the older individuals came to my aid, showing me how to tie it in a manner that eased the burden on my head.

I cherish the memories of visiting the farm to harvest and savor crops like watermelons and cucumbers that we had cultivated ourselves. Additionally, there were unforgettable moments, particularly during holidays such as Christmas or New Year's, when the founders allowed the older members to slaughter some of the pigs for us to feast on. Since meat was a rarity in our daily diet, these occasions felt incredibly special and were moments of genuine joy and celebration for all of us.

Life at the mission transcended the routine of daily tasks, studies, and prayers. Each day presented an opportunity for personal growth, for gaining wisdom, and for self-reflection. My time there was not just a phase, but a pivotal moment—a period that taught me the essence of resilience, faith, and perseverance. The lessons I absorbed during those crucial years have shaped my identity, instilling within me a sense of purpose and a profound appreciation for the virtues of diligence, community, and altruism. This journey, with its blend of hardships and victories, has left an indelible imprint on my character, forever guiding my path ahead.

I aspire for my journey to serve as a beacon of hope for those weathering their storms. For within the depths of hardship and despair, we unearth our inner strength. In the face of adversity, hope emerges as a steadfast companion. And amidst the anguish of loss, we discover the resilience to press onward. The fortitude forged in the crucible of adversity becomes our greatest ally, propelling us forward, even when the road ahead appears daunting and arduous.

As I stand at the intersection of my past and future, I am filled with reflection on the journey that has molded me into the person

I am today, while also embracing the anticipation of a future ripe with opportunities for evolution and advancement. I gaze back at the mission, a place that sometimes felt like a crucible of strict discipline and consequences, yet also served as a nurturing and formative environment.

As I contemplate the principles upheld by the mission founders and my parents, it becomes evident that their beliefs were shaped by the context of their era and surroundings. In their worldview, discipline was synonymous with sternness and inflexibility—an essential tool for shaping youthful minds and character. This approach was entrenched in their beliefs and values; it constituted their reality. However, they operated within the constraints of their time, devoid of the insights into child psychology and effective methods of fostering positive behavior that we possess today. Their intentions were noble, driven by a desire to provide what they deemed best for us, yet their methodologies were limited by their knowledge and resources.

Today, my journey has led me to the citadels of knowledge and enlightenment, where I've been fortunate to acquire a different perspective. I've come to realize that corporal punishment isn't the most effective means of instilling discipline in a child. Modern research emphasizes the significance of positive reinforcement in fostering good behavior and highlights the detrimental effects of physical punishment (Kazdin, 2013). Creating a nurturing and supportive environment, alongside utilizing praise and rewards to reinforce desirable conduct, has been demonstrated to yield superior outcomes in shaping a child's character. However, this insight wasn't available to the founders of the mission during my time there. They lived in an era where corporal punishment was regarded as essential, the ultimate disciplinary tool. Their understanding was molded by the prevailing societal norms and values of their era.

It's crucial to recognize that knowledge is dynamic; it evolves as we learn and gain new experiences. Knowledge empowers us, and a lack of it can lead to decisions we may later question. Now, armed with the understanding I've gained, I can recognize the shortcomings in their approach. Yet, I also empathize with why they made those decisions, believing they were acting in our best interests. In my current position, equipped with this knowledge and insight, I perceive an opportunity—a chance to make a difference, to break the cycle. Despite its imperfections, the mission has endowed me with strength and determination. With these attributes and the knowledge, I've acquired, I possess a unique opportunity to effect change.

I can utilize my understanding and experiences to contribute to the creation of environments where children are nurtured with love and patience. Instead of resorting to harsh punishment, they can be guided towards discipline through positive reinforcement. Additionally, I can share my journey as evidence that change is not only feasible but imperative. By assimilating lessons from the past and applying our current knowledge, we can collectively strive toward a future that is characterized by kindness, empathy, and support.

REFLECTIONS AND LESSONS

The last day at the mission symbolized both closure and commencement—a moment akin to reaching the final page of an engrossing novel. As I stood at the threshold, suitcase in hand, my heart resonated with a whirlwind of emotions. Casting a fleeting glance back at the structure that had served as both haven and confinement, I pondered the transformative odyssey that had shaped me. No longer was I the timid, rebellious boy who had arrived at its gates. In his stead stood a resolute teenager, molded by challenges, camaraderie, and personal growth, poised to unravel the mysteries of the world beyond.

Going back to Mamba Point was like going back to where I started. Everything felt familiar—every street, every face, even the smells in the air—they all reminded me of my past. It was where I used to dream big dreams, with nothing to hold me back and a spirit too big for limits. But now, I came back not as that rebellious kid, but as a young man with dreams and duties to carry.

Reuniting with my family was a whirlwind of emotions—joy, relief, and a strong sense of pride. They recognized in me the same innocent child who had left, now back, shaped by life's experiences but still fundamentally the same at heart.

In the days that followed, I wrestled with conflicting feelings. The strict discipline enforced by the mission occasionally felt like chains, yet at other times, it provided the stability I needed amidst life's unpredictability. My once rebellious spirit had evolved, still fiery but now tempered with a wisdom that aimed to comprehend rather than solely defy.

My friendship with Junior had a profound impact on me during my time at the mission. His passing served as a poignant reminder of life's fleeting nature. It motivated me to seize each moment, to love without reservation, and to strive to make a positive difference in the world, just as he had done for me.

As I transitioned from adolescence to adulthood, the lessons imparted by the mission became beacons of guidance. The stringent routine that once felt stifling now provided a structure for accountability, and the solitude that once felt isolating taught me the value of self-reliance. The relationships forged during my time there emphasized the significance of authentic connections.

Looking back on this journey, I see it as a gradual process of growth—a mixture of learning, letting go of old beliefs, and adopting new ones. It required acknowledging my shortcomings, embracing my imperfections, and striving for improvement. This ongoing journey has molded me into the person I am today, leaving a lasting impression on my character.

As the saying goes, it's in the midst of storms that our true selves emerge. It's this resilience, this unwavering spirit, forged in the fires of adversity, that has been my compass, guiding me from the turbulent times at the mission and propelling me forward on life's journey. I've come to realize that transformation isn't a fixed point but an ongoing voyage, and I'm grateful for every step of this path.

FAMILY DISRUPTION

My reentry into the world outside the mission was not a grand event with ceremonies or festivities. Instead, it was a quiet, understated transition, filled with a blend of emotions—sadness, confusion, and anticipation. I had envisioned leaving the mission as liberating, an entrance into a realm brimming with possibilities. However, the unforeseen dissolution of my family brought a sense of sorrow and disillusionment to my newfound freedom. The warm embrace of home that I yearned for was replaced by a cold sense of emptiness.

My father's dreams have long been the thread that weaves through our family's story, his visions radiant with hope as he imagined our future dwelling in a tranquil sanctuary, far removed from the hustle and bustle of city life. However, the reality we lived starkly diverged from these lofty aspirations, underscoring the disparity between dreams and the harshness of our circumstances. This dissonance echoed my evolution, from a rebellious youth to someone molded by the discipline of the mission.

Time has a way of reshaping life, often fragmenting what was once a cohesive family unit. This transformation was spurred by my father's decision to build his home on a piece of land inherited from my grandfather and shared among him and his siblings. However, this move was not devoid of challenges, as it occurred amidst ongoing property disputes that had already claimed the lives of other family members. Furthermore, lingering memories from my early years in my grandfather's home cast a shadow over this decision. Opting for solitude, my father chose to reside alone in the house he constructed in Paynesville. Situated on a plot passed down from my grandfather, this residence stood as one of the few assets he could rightfully claim. Notably, it remained unaffected by the disputes and threats associated with his stepmother's claims, providing him with a haven free from such turmoil.

Caught between the realms of childhood and adulthood, I found myself yearning for the unity of our past while simultaneously recognizing my growth. The fractured family dynamic served as a mirror to the intricate facets of my identity.

Resilience became ingrained, not suddenly, but as a trait honed over time. The house in Paynesville came to symbolize my journey and the unwavering spirit that guided us along divergent paths.

This shattered reality signified not an end, but rather a pivotal juncture, deepening my journey of self-discovery. Intertwined with my evolution, my family's narrative unfolded as a tale replete with love, ambition, conflict, and resolution—a saga that I continued to navigate and embrace.

Resilience, forged through adversity, propelled me onward, fortified by the understanding that I had emerged stronger from life's trials. The challenges faced at the mission and within the complexities of my fragmented family provided a solid foundation for my future pursuits.

My story is one of contrasts and personal growth, from the bustling noise of city life to the tranquil peace of the mission, from the bonds of familial unity to the solitary path of individual development. Through these diverse experiences, I learned valuable lessons in resilience, determination, and the continuous pursuit of self-improvement.

The Paynesville home evolved from being a representation of my father's steadfast dream to a testament of resilience and faith in one's aspirations. It became a symbol of our family's trials and triumphs, embodying the resilience and inner strength that each of us possessed.

Recognizing that transformation is an ongoing journey rather than a final destination, I found gratitude in the myriad experiences that molded me. I saw echoes of myself mirrored in both my parents—the practicality of my mother and my father's unwavering determination to chase his dreams. This introspection allowed me to acknowledge my personal growth and to embrace the possibilities for further development in the future.

This narrative, woven with threads of love, ambition, and resilience, unveiled the depth of my inner strength. Every interaction with my parents and moment of self-reflection fortified me, illuminating our individual yet interconnected journeys of resilience and perseverance.

Despite the uncertainties and challenges of the world beyond my immediate surroundings, I had undergone growth and transformation, navigating a path toward self-discovery amidst the intricate complexities of life.

As I navigated the aftermath of my mission experience and grappled with the complexities of my familial circumstances, I relied on the lessons learned as my compass, continuously evolving within the intricate mosaic of my family's narrative.

In life, every part matters. My journey had ups and downs, but it shows how strong we can be and how life goes on. My story is like a picture waiting for me to be brave and keep going, painting a future full of hope and dreams.

OUTBREAK OF THE SECOND LIBERIAN CIVIL WAR

Imagine a sunny day suddenly turning dark as storm clouds roll in, the brightness of the sun replaced by the ominous sight of thunder and lightning. That's how war came to Liberia. One moment, we were kids playing marbles on the streets, innocent and carefree. The next, we were huddled in fear, listening to the frightening sounds of gunfire and sirens, our hearts racing.

This chapter explores one of the toughest times in my life—the start of the second Liberian Civil War. It was a difficult period that, despite the hardships, changed how I see the world.

The war wasn't just something that happened—it was like a storm that completely altered our lives. We lost people we loved, our homes were destroyed, and our childhoods were taken away from us. These painful experiences stayed with us, deeply ingrained in our memories and feelings. The war made us face our fears and worries head-on. The sound of gunfire, the sight of violence, and the constant uncertainty—it felt like we were fighting a battle every single day. It was during this time that I discovered the strength inside me, the bravery to face my fears and to see beyond them.

This chapter isn't just about the hardships of war, but also about the rise of resilience, the wisdom we gained, and the inner strength we uncovered in tough times. So, as we continue forward, let's keep in mind that after every storm, there's a rainbow, and after every dark night, there's the hope of a new day.

The new millennium was supposed to bring a sense of new beginnings, a chance for renewal, and hope for stability after the troubles of the past. But in Liberia, things turned out quite differently from what we had hoped for.

In September 2000, our troubled past returned to haunt us. Rebels and government forces clashed violently in the North. The fear of war, a haunting specter we knew all too well, once again loomed over the nation like a dark cloud.

Monrovia, our resilient capital city, stood as a testament to the wounds of years of conflict. Every morning, we faced a city marked by its tumultuous history—fallen buildings, broken streets, and a pervasive sense of fear that had become part of our daily existence. However, on that ominous Monday morning, the atmosphere was distinct. An eerie silence filled the air, hinting at the approaching storm.

Amidst the broken streets of Monrovia, crowds of Liberians gathered at Graystone camp, an American compound towering opposite the United States embassy. Graystone camp had become a familiar refuge for thousands of Liberians during the war. On the other side of its imposing fences, American diplomats and the global community watched with deep disappointment. They had issued warnings during the 1997 elections, warnings that proved valid. These warnings stemmed from the harrowing experiences of commanders and rebels during the 1989-1990 war. Their subsequent rule was characterized by chaos and instability.

Despite these warnings, the Liberian people made their choice in July 1997, while the world watched. The complex interplay of political realities, combined with the nation's desperate longing for stability, influenced this decision. However, the consequences of this choice soon became painfully evident. The ominous shadow of war had returned, dashing our hopes for peace and stability. Liberia teetered on the brink of yet another devastating conflict: the second Liberian Civil War, a brutal struggle that would range from 1999 to 2003. The failure of post-first civil war transitional processes, such as disarmament, demobilization, rehabilitation, and reintegration, as well as security sector reform, fueled this conflict (Kieh, 2009). This complex web of strife was further divided into three distinct yet interconnected wars, locally known as War 1, War 2, and War 3.

I remember the moment when the school bell rang earlier than usual, its solemn sound echoing the seriousness of the situation. The teachers, normally calm and composed, looked worried. The school hallways, usually lively with chatter, were now filled with quiet whispers and a heavy silence. We were dismissed from school earlier than expected. I can still vividly recall my mother's arrival. Her usually warm eyes were filled with concern. As she hugged me tightly, I could feel her heart beating fast, matching the chaos around us. She held my hand firmly, as if afraid I might slip away. Despite her attempts to reassure me with a smile, I could hear the fear in her voice. That day, our familiar world was changing, and we stood on the edge, watching as a storm approached, threatening to engulf everything we held dear.

I remember the day vividly when we received the distressing news. Around mid-2003, rebel forces had taken over a third of northern Liberia and were nearing the capital. Monrovia was besieged, with rebel groups continuously shelling the city (BBC News Africa, 2002). The announcement spread fear throughout the city like ripples in water.

In just moments, our peaceful city was turned upside down. The once quiet streets were now filled with scared civilians. Monrovia, which had enjoyed a brief period of calm, was now threatened by war once more. The peace we had cherished was suddenly shattered. Our lives changed drastically. We had to face the harsh reality of survival, resistance, and the struggle to hold onto hope. The peaceful moments we once knew were replaced by a new normal, where every day was a fight for survival. With heavy hearts and uncertain minds, we prepared ourselves for the impending war, knowing it would be a tough and relentless battle.

During those days, a strange sense of déjà vu engulfed me. Monrovia, once bustling with life and activity, now resembled a vast chessboard. Invisible forces manipulated the pieces, engaging in a game of power, control, and dominance. Every move in the city, every change in dynamics, mirrored the intricate strategies of this high-stakes game, where the city and its inhabitants were mere pawns.

Amidst my thoughts and emotions, I struggled to make sense of the rapidly evolving situation. The once clear blue sky, a reflection of my boundless dreams, was now obscured by dark clouds of war. This change in the city's atmosphere mirrored our collective unease, a tangible manifestation of the fear that gripped every aspect of our lives. News of the conflicts in Monrovia spread swiftly, heightening uncertainty and dread. Whispers of war echoed through the bustling markets, the quiet corners of our schools, and the hushed conversations at home. Despite our efforts to ignore the looming threat, its presence was impossible to escape.

Despite the looming shadow of war, life continued in its peculiar and resilient fashion. Our daily routines remained, occasionally disrupted by updates on the escalating conflict. This was our way of coping, of reclaiming a semblance of normalcy amidst the chaos. However, beneath the surface of our everyday lives, an undeniable sense of fear and anticipation lingered. We all waited anxiously, holding our breath, scanning the horizon for any signs of the impending storm.

Our home mirrored the atmosphere of the city. My mother, a symbol of strength and resilience, tried to maintain a sense of normalcy in our daily lives. She masked her worries with a brave smile, her quiet determination providing us with a sense of security in the face of impending war. Our home, once a haven of warmth and tranquility, now became a fortress, a refuge against the storm looming outside. The sounds of laughter and shared stories that once filled our space were replaced by quiet conversations and whispered prayers. We clung to hope, holding onto each other tightly as we prepared for what lay ahead, uncertain of what the future held.

As days passed and weeks turned into months, the rumors of war became a stark reality. The simmering tension erupted into full-scale conflict, plunging the nation into another war. The sound of gunfire became a grim backdrop, the violent rhythm accompanying our daily existence. The bustling city fell into a haunting silence, broken only by sporadic shelling and gunfire. Monrovia reverted to a war zone once more.

Faced with this violent reality, we resorted to what we knew best—we persevered. We found strength in each other, in our shared hopes and fears, and in our collective resilience. Though the shadow of war cast a dark pall over our city, our homes, and our lives, it could not extinguish the flicker of hope in our hearts. Amidst the chaos and devastation, we sought solace in unity, drew strength from shared struggles, and clung to hope in our resilience.

SEEKING SANCTUARY

I have vivid memories of the first time my family and I sought refuge at Graystone. It was a mix of fear, desperation, and relief that I will never forget. It happened on April 6, 1996, during the war. However, when the second civil war broke out, we attempted to use the same strategy for safety, but unfortunately, it didn't work as effectively. Graystone became our sanctuary. Its sturdy structure, fortified gates, and reputation for security attracted Liberians seeking shelter from the war. I recall everyone in our household hurriedly packing their belongings, preparing to move there. As one of the older children, I was selected to accompany a group of teenagers while our parents finished packing at home.

The scene at Graystone was incredibly chaotic. Many Liberians, gripped by fear and desperation, congregated at the entrance. Initially, the gates were locked, but they eventually gave way under the pressure of the frightened crowd. I witnessed some brave individuals scaling the walls, ignoring the sharp barbed wires on top. It was a frantic scramble for safety, highlighting the extremes people would go to in order to protect themselves and their loved ones. Once the gates were breached, families and individuals streamed in, each striving to secure their place. We found a spot and anxiously awaited the reunion with our parents. We settled in, organizing our belongings, including mattresses for rest and pots and dishes for meal preparation. We believed we were safe, sheltered from the war unfolding outside.

I remember feeling a sense of relief that day. Unfortunately, that feeling of safety didn't last long. The relationship between the Liberian people and their American protectors started to deteriorate. During the 1997 elections, Liberians elected a leader against the strong advice of the Americans. In response, the Americans withdrew their support, removing the security measures that had once protected us and preventing civilians from entering Graystone.

After we had settled in initially, a group of us teenagers ventured out to find some food. Despite the tense situation, the atmosphere inside Graystone was surprisingly pleasant. People were cooking, selling food, chatting, and trying to carry on with life as best as they could given the circumstances. As we made our way back to our spot with food in hand, the tranquility was shattered by the terrifying sound of an explosion.

The peace we had briefly found within Graystone was shattered in an instant. Screams and cries filled the air as a second explosion rang out, even louder than the first. Chaos erupted as people rushed to gather their belongings and move deeper into the compound, while others decided to leave altogether.

I was stunned, standing in the aftermath of the explosion that had narrowly missed me. Just a few minutes earlier, I had been at the very spot where the first rocket had landed. A man ran past me, his hands cut off from the blast, bloodied and in shock. A tree had been uprooted entirely, its roots naked in the smoke-filled air. As I looked around, the shocking sight of families that had previously been lying on their mattresses now lay lifeless—women, children, men, young and old alike. Body parts were scattered everywhere, and the injured were crying out in pain.

The teens who had gone with me to acquire lunch had drifted apart in the subsequent panic. Bewildered and afraid, they ran to their parents' house. My mother informed me afterward that the news had completely overwhelmed her. Tears were running down her cheeks as she hurriedly looked for me. As soon as word of the explosion spread, many friends and family members raced to Graystone to see how their loved ones were doing.

The reunion with my mother was filled with emotion. We were

both shaken but relieved to be together and safe. As we exited the complex, we were confronted with a devastating scene. Dead bodies lay scattered across the ground, and we had to step carefully to avoid them. Outside, people were crying and searching desperately for their loved ones, hoping they were not among the casualties. Workers were loading bodies onto trucks for burial, and the grim reality of the tragedy hit us hard. Writing about this part of my life forces me to pause often. My heart races, and I need to take deep breaths to calm myself before continuing. The memories of that day continue to haunt me, serving as a stark reminder of the horrors of war.

Looking back on our experiences, I can't help but recall all the times war forced us to leave our homes and seek safety elsewhere. It feels like we're reliving the same story, finding ourselves displaced once again because Graystone camp, our latest refuge, was no longer safe. With heavy hearts and knowing we had no other option, we journeyed from Monrovia to Duala and New Kru Town. It was a long walk, nearly four hours, but each step was fueled by our desperate hope for safety and a semblance of peace amidst the chaos.

The terrifying events of that day left a permanent mark on my mind. I had to mature quickly, facing situations of life and death that no child should ever have to experience. The days after the incident passed in a blur of shock and numbness. The memories of the chaos, the desperate cries, the scent of blood, and the sight of lifeless bodies haunted me relentlessly. My mother, showing remarkable strength, remained by my side, guiding me through the turmoil and encouraging me to be courageous.

In the days and weeks that followed, life became a blur of survival tasks. Despite the shock and pain, we had to press on. We scoured for food, searched for shelter, and prioritized our safety. Each day was consumed by these urgent needs, overshadowed by the constant fear and anxiety that loomed over us.

During that period, I encountered remarkable individuals who, despite the harrowing circumstances, displayed remarkable strength, resilience, and unwavering determination. Together, we forged an unspoken bond, united by our shared experiences. We leaned on each other for support, sharing whatever resources we had, and offering solace in times of distress. Through our collective struggle, we discovered the resilience of the human spirit and the remarkable capacity to find hope amidst despair. These individuals became my extended family, teaching me invaluable lessons about endurance, solidarity, and the enduring power of hope.

As time passed, the conflict escalated, plunging the vibrant city of Monrovia into desolation. Once bustling streets now lay deserted, engulfed in an eerie silence broken only by distant gunfire and the occasional explosion of mortar shells. Despite the looming danger and pervasive uncertainty, we clung to hope, believing that brighter days lay ahead.

One day, the news arrived like a ray of hope: a ceasefire had been declared. A surge of relief flooded through me, releasing the tension I had been holding onto for so long. It felt like I had been holding my breath, and finally, I could exhale. The fighting had ceased, but the wounds of war ran deep. The city lay in ruins, the economy was in shambles, and the toll on human lives was immeasurable.

Gradually, we started rebuilding our shattered lives. The markets reopened, schools resumed classes, and a sense of routine began to return. However, the specter of war lingered, casting a long shadow over our daily lives. Every noise made us jump, every unfamiliar face sparked fear. The trauma of war had deeply scarred us, leaving wounds that would take years, perhaps even a lifetime, to fully heal.

Walking through the devastated streets of Monrovia, I couldn't shake the feeling of profound loss. We had survived the war, but it had taken its toll. The city I once cherished was now a mere shell of its former self. The lively neighborhoods were now eerily quiet, devoid of the laughter and camaraderie that once filled the air.

Instead, there was a palpable sense of grief and fear that hung over everything like a dark cloud.

Despite the despair, a glimmer of hope ignited within me. Despite the horrors we endured, I believed in our ability to rebuild. Like a phoenix rising from the ashes, we could emerge from this darkness stronger and more resilient. The war had robbed us of much, but it had also instilled in us a profound appreciation for peace, unity, and resilience. While the road ahead would be challenging, I remained confident that together, we could overcome any obstacle.

Looking back on my life, I'm amazed by the incredible resilience and inner strength we humans possess. I stand as living proof of that resilience. I survived a brutal war that shattered my world, took my loved ones, and forced me to mature beyond my years. Yet, I endured. I emerged from the darkness, and if I could, then anyone can. While my journey continues, I'm committed to using my experiences to make a difference, to promote peace, and to amplify the voices of survivors.

In conclusion, my life story is one of survival, resilience, and hope. It's the story of a young boy thrust into adulthood by the brutal realities of war, who emerged from the darkness with newfound strength. If I could endure the horrors of war, I could face any challenge. Remember, even in the darkest of times, there is always a glimmer of hope. Keep that hope alive and never lose faith in the indomitable power of the human spirit.

A FIGHT FOR EDUCATION

Growing up in post-war Liberia felt like walking through a minefield, every step held the potential for hardship, and every choice could alter my path. As I reached my teenage years, life in Monrovia, the capital city, became a daily battle for survival. I faced the typical struggles of adolescence but against the backdrop of a city still reeling from conflict. Identity crises, rebellion, and the longing for independence took on new significance amidst poverty and a troubled past.

I recall feeling overwhelmed, like a square peg trying to fit into a round hole. My defiance surged, and in typical teenage rebellion, I frequently tested my mother's patience. Fueled by an insatiable thirst for change, I impulsively packed my bags one day and moved in with my father and stepmother.

Life at my father's was anything but easy. It was filled with hardships and struggles. While the environment was calmer compared to Monrovia, it presented its challenges. Affording school fees became a constant battle, and more often than not, it was my mother who had to step in to assist, despite her limited resources, as my father's business struggled in the tough economy. This transition served as a harsh reality check, but with time, I adapted. Fueled by a determination to continue my education, I managed to enroll in Paynesville Central Academy (PCA), a public school in Paynesville City, keeping my educational aspirations alive.

Attaining an education wasn't guaranteed; it was a privilege that many couldn't afford. The struggle to pay school fees grew more daunting with each passing day. Motivated by desperation and a passion for learning, I navigated the rough streets of Paynesville, selling kerosene from door to door to earn money for my school fees and other necessities.

The burden of survival was always on my shoulders, but so was my unwavering determination. I remember being sent home from school many times because of unpaid fees, but each setback only made me more determined. Sometimes, I would sneak into the examination hall through the backdoor ceiling, my heart pounding with the fear of being caught and the eagerness to learn, all while hoping that my parents would soon be able to afford the fees.

Despite the challenges, my passion for education never waned. I remained committed, even in the face of adversity. I continuously pleaded with school administrators, asking them to allow me to attend classes and take my exams. Sometimes, my efforts paid off, but other times, I faced only rejection and disappointment.

The challenges I faced may have been what drove me forward. I rose to leadership roles, serving as class president at both Paynesville Central Academy (PCA) and George Toe Washington School, and later at Jimmy Jillocon High School. These positions, though demanding, taught me invaluable lessons. They reinforced my determination to succeed, solidifying my belief in my capabilities and paving the way for my future pursuits.

Amidst these experiences, one desire remained steadfast—a silent yearning to cross the Atlantic and pursue a better life and education in the United States. The prospect of realizing this dream felt as distant as the land itself. I couldn't fathom the how or when, yet I held onto a glimmer of hope, a beacon in the surrounding darkness. And then, against all odds, it happened.

As I write these words, I'm struck by the remarkable journey I've traveled. My story speaks to the resilience of the human spirit, which persists even in the most challenging circumstances. My struggle wasn't just about surviving the aftermath of the Liberian Civil War or navigating the trials of adolescence. It was about pursuing a better life, advocating for my education, and refusing to let circumstances define my future.

In the midst of unyielding hardship, my days in Paynesville were characterized by resilience. Despite the challenges, I discovered moments of happiness in the friendships I cultivated at school. These companions were more than just friends; they were my fellow soldiers in the struggle of life, allies who shared in the bitterness of adversity and the sweetness of small victories.

Selling kerosene, a laborious and sometimes demeaning task, became a vital aspect of my life. Journeying long distances along winding paths and rough roads, knocking on strangers' doors, encountering apathy, and occasionally contempt, I hustled for every cent. Despite its challenges, this experience served as a lesson in perseverance, reminding me daily of the daunting obstacles I faced, and the determination needed to confront them head-on.

The school, despite its indifference to my financial struggles, became a refuge—a sanctuary that, in its peculiar manner, nourished my aspirations and ambitions. With each silent entry into the school's grounds, my resolve strengthened. Every class I attended, every exam I managed to sit for, represented a modest triumph in my ongoing struggle.

During moments of profound desperation, I often questioned the validity of my struggle. The prospect of a better life in the United States appeared as a distant vision, forever beyond my grasp. Yet, despite the overwhelming odds, I held onto the hope of realizing that dream. It served as sustenance for my aspirations, a beacon guiding me through the darkest moments of my reality.

Setting foot in the United States felt like entering a dream. The land I had longed for, once seemingly beyond reach, now lay beneath my feet. This transition signaled the beginning of a new chapter in my life, one brimming with novel challenges, unexplored opportunities, and an unfamiliar terrain.

As I reflect on my life's journey, I'm reminded of countless others who have been shaped by similar experiences. I think of the numerous children whose innocence has been shattered by the horrors of war, the resilient survivors navigating the aftermath of conflict, and the determined dreamers who refuse to let their circumstances dictate their futures.

By sharing my journey, I aim to inspire others with my story, to ignite a flame in their hearts, and to reassure them that no dream is too distant, no obstacle too insurmountable, and no path too arduous. The human spirit is indomitable, and it possesses the ability to turn aspirations into achievements.

REFLECTION AND PURPOSE

Experiencing the devastating civil war completely transformed my life. As a child, I confronted a reality where even the smallest actions could determine life or death. My innocence was stripped away, and I was forced to acquire survival skills at a tender age. The Liberian Civil War served as an unwanted teacher, imparting harsh lessons about the fragility of life. It was an education devoid of traditional classrooms, textbooks, and chalkboards, but instead filled with the daily agony and anguish we endured. For a long time, I buried these memories deep within me, hoping to never revisit them. However, there comes a point when silence becomes burdensome, and concealing my past becomes unbearable. That moment arrived when I began to share my life story.

Writing about my past was a difficult and emotionally challenging endeavor. Each word and sentence I penned felt like a sharp blade, unearthing the painful memories I had long attempted to bury. At times, the emotions threatened to engulf me, but I persisted because I recognized that this journey of recounting my past was about more than just myself.

My story stands as a testament to the resilience of the human spirit, honoring the countless innocent lives torn apart by the ravages of war. It echoes the silent cries of every child whose joyous laughter was drowned out by the thunderous blasts of gunfire and whose playgrounds were tragically transformed into fields of conflict. This memoir serves as a beacon of hope amidst the darkest despair, showcasing the indomitable resilience that emerges in the face of unimaginable horror, and the remarkable ability to persevere even when the odds appear insurmountable.

As I revisited the traumas of the Liberian Civil War, a peculiar feeling of gratitude washed over me. Yes, it may sound surprising, but

I am indeed grateful—not for the war itself or the pain it brought, but for the invaluable lessons it imparted. Despite its devastating impact, the civil war became a harsh yet effective teacher, instilling within me an unwavering spirit of resilience and perseverance. It taught me the importance of clinging to hope even in the darkest of times and demonstrated that the human spirit possesses an inherent strength that can withstand even the direst of circumstances.

Documenting my experiences and trauma proved to be a form of therapy for me. It became my way of bringing order to the chaos that had profoundly shaped my life. By laying bare the wounds of my past, I gradually began to perceive them not as mere reminders of my pain, but as testaments to my resilience. These scars transformed into badges of honor, proof that I had faced adversity head-on and emerged from it with newfound strength.

It's widely acknowledged that not everyone who undergoes trauma develops Post-Traumatic Stress Disorder (PTSD), and I am a living example of this phenomenon. Research in the field supports this idea, suggesting that resilience, or the ability to adapt to traumatic events, plays a crucial role in determining whether one develops PTSD symptoms (Rutter, 1985). Despite the traumatic events I've faced, I've been able to build a life that isn't defined by those experiences, but rather by my resilience and inner strength.

Looking back on my childhood, I can't help but acknowledge the paradox of my upbringing. I was born into a period of apparent tranquility and progress, just before the outbreak of the civil war. During this time, Liberia was hailed as a symbol of stability in Africa, boasting top-tier hospitals, schools, and robust infrastructure—a time fondly remembered as the "Normal Days."

In my early years, everything was peaceful and calm. But when the Liberian Civil War started, things changed fast. I was just a kid, so I didn't get how serious it was. But I remember my parents being scared and confused when they heard about the war. Schools closed, and the streets, which used to be busy, got quiet. It was like everything we knew was gone, replaced by the sound of gunfire. My parents did their best to keep me safe during the war. They stayed strong and gave us hope, even when things seemed bad.

Writing about these experiences felt like reliving them. Each word I wrote brought back a rush of memories, making my past feel more real than my present. It was emotionally exhausting, as I had to confront the difficult parts of my past. However, I kept going because I felt a responsibility to share my story and shed light on the terrible realities of war.

As I delved deeper into my past, I also thought about resilience. Resilience has always been a part of my life, something my parents taught me during and after the war. They showed me how to be strong and keep going. To me, resilience means more than just surviving. It means having the strength to face challenges and thrive despite the odds.

The war still affects me deeply, and the scars I carry are a reminder of the hardships I endured. But I wear these scars proudly because they show the resilience, I discovered within myself during those difficult times. It was during the war and struggles that I learned the power of hope, the strength of the human spirit, and the incredible ability to bounce back.

In sharing my story, I also hope to raise awareness about the harsh realities of war, to inspire empathy, and to invoke action. The atrocities of war should not be hidden away; they should be exposed, discussed, and addressed. Only then can we hope to build a world that is free from conflict, a world where every child has the right to a peaceful childhood. We must come together to stand up against war and violence, to strive for justice, and to create a better future for all. It is only through our collective action that we can make the world a better place for everyone.

The Journey to Hope

My path from Liberia's shadows to the pursuit of hope in a new world is a testament to the courage required to embrace change. This chapter reflects my journey toward stability and self-discovery, marking the beginning of my quest for a brighter future.

3

A New Dawn

> "HOPE IS BEING ABLE TO SEE THAT THERE IS LIGHT DESPITE ALL OF THE DARKNESS." - DESMOND TUTU

With the dawn comes new light, new hope, and new beginnings. The third chapter of my journey, "A New Dawn," unfolds this transformative phase of my life when I found myself boarding a plane, crossing oceans, and stepping onto a land that held the promise of a better tomorrow - America.

This chapter is about transitions and adjustments, about embracing the unfamiliar and challenging the odd. It's a narrative of a young man navigating his way through the web of cultural differences, language barriers, and the daunting journey of carving out a space for himself in a new world.

It's also a tale of resilience. It tells the story of a boy from Liberia who makes peace with his past, embraces his present, and envisions a future that leads him to pursue education and a meaningful life.

As we journey through "A New Dawn," you'll witness the first glimmers of hope breaking through the shadows of my past, illuminating my path and guiding me toward a world filled with possibilities. It was in this unfamiliar landscape that I began to grasp the power of transformation and discover the strength within me.

May 8, 2008, a date that stirs up mixed feelings, marked the day my mother, sister, and I bid farewell to our homeland. Departing from Robert's International Airport, we took to the skies, our hearts burdened yet hopeful as we embarked on a new beginning in the United States.

From the moment we landed, we were strangers in a foreign land. A new culture awaited us to decode, a language to master, and customs to comprehend. Each step forward felt like navigating a path scattered with unseen thorns, laden with challenges. Yet, this chapter isn't solely about those hurdles. It's about clinging to hope and maneuvering through setbacks and obstacles that cross our path.

DEPARTURE FROM HOMELAND

May 8, 2008, remains imprinted in my heart—an unforgettable day, tinged with the bittersweet farewell that clings to me like a shadow. Standing on the tarmac at Robert's International Airport, my emotions were swift. Departing Liberia was painful; it felt like leaving a piece of myself behind. Yet, at the same time, I was moving towards something new in the United States—a chance at the life I had always envisioned. Excitement pulsed through me for the possibilities ahead, but fear also crept in. Fear of making mistakes, fear of disappointing my resilient family. My mother's words, "Never forget where you come from," echoed in my mind, guiding me as I braved this monumental leap.

In the days before my departure, my family overwhelmed me with advice. My grandma, with her sage wisdom, cautioned me to avoid trouble. Other relatives echoed similar sentiments, urging me not to disgrace the family, recounting tales of young men who had strayed in the States. The weight of their words was heavy. Even one of my aunts proposed to my mom that perhaps someone else should go ahead of me, questioning my readiness—a suggestion my mom outright dismissed.

To be frank, the realization that some people were betting on my failure stung deeply. It seemed unjust, particularly from those who didn't truly know me. However, rather than letting it weigh me down, I turned it into motivation. I resolved to prove everyone wrong, especially myself. I was determined to demonstrate that I wasn't the person they doubted. My primary goal was to make my family proud.

Life has a strange way of tossing curveballs our way, but with a touch of faith, I found my way through the unfamiliar world I landed in. Admittedly, there were bumps along the road, mistakes were made, and lessons learned the hard way. Nevertheless, I persevered. Perfection wasn't my aim; it was growth. And grow I did, steadily but surely, transforming doubts into tales of triumph.

I may not be perfect—not even close—but I've made significant strides. Against all odds, I've forged a life here, demonstrating to my family, and perhaps most significantly, to myself, that I am capable. My journey serves as a poignant reminder that it's not about your starting point but rather your destination and the person you evolve into along the way.

The United States, starkly different from Liberia, welcomed us as a gigantic melting pot of cultures, traditions, and societal norms. My mother, sister, and I confronted the daunting task of assimilation. We dove headfirst into adapting to this new environment—grappling with the American accent, or as we fondly referred to it back in Liberia, the "Series," navigating unfamiliar societal customs, and adapting to an education system far more advanced than what we were accustomed to.

Our transition into this new life was fraught with unforeseen challenges and obstacles. The narrative of our emigration stands as a testament to our resilience in the face of adversity and our steadfast determination to cling to hope, even amidst the most daunting circumstances.

Upon arrival, I felt as though I had regressed in my educational journey. Despite having completed eleventh grade in Liberia, I found myself placed in eleventh grade in the United States due to disparities between the Liberian and American education systems, compounded by incomplete school documents. This reassignment felt like a setback, shaking my confidence and faith in my abilities.

Rather than giving in to disappointment, I embraced this challenge with grace and humility. I held onto the belief that education was the key, the equalizer that would push me toward the future I dreamed of. It became my stepping-stone toward reaching the American Dream, which now seemed tantalizingly within reach.

I enrolled at Memorial High School and moved in with my aunt to be within the school district. Her apartment, just a short walk from the school, became my new base. The school was a melting pot of cultures, languages, and customs, providing a daily dose of new experiences. Amidst this diversity, I felt both fascination and intimidation, but I embraced it all as part of my growth journey. Choosing my classes and preparing for college was overwhelming, but I was fortunate to have Mrs. Gaddis, as my high school counselor. She was like an angel sent from heaven, helping me navigate the difficulties of being new and confused. Her guidance eased my anxieties and significantly helped me settle in. Mrs. Gaddis was one of the individuals who inspired me to work in the school system as an embedded mental health therapist.

Life in the U.S. unfolded like a tapestry of experiences, each thread weaving a story of struggle and triumph. While some students teased me for being an "African boy," others extended their friendship, gradually enlarging my small circle of friends.

As days melted into weeks and weeks stretched into months, every moment transformed into a lesson in patience, resilience, and perseverance. The academic hurdles and language barriers frequently felt insurmountable, yet the aspiration for a better life and the pursuit of the American Dream anchored my focus.

Beyond academics, adapting to cultural differences presented an additional layer of challenges. Observing the harmonious coexistence of diverse cultures was both intriguing and enlightening, imparting lessons in acceptance, tolerance, and adaptability.

Throughout these challenges, my family's support remained steadfast. This journey of adaptation proved humbling, teaching me to embrace the unknown, learn from mistakes, and remain undeterred by setbacks. I realized that each step, no matter how arduous, shaped me into a stronger, more resilient individual. This resilience, honed over time, has become my shield in life.

Reflecting on my journey from Liberia to the United States, it's evident that it was punctuated by trials, yet these experiences have molded me into the person I am today. My story, intertwined with those of countless other immigrants pursuing the American Dream, serves as a testament to our indomitable spirit, resilience, and unwavering hope for a brighter future.

4

The Guiding Light

"IN THE MIDST OF DARKNESS, LIGHT PERSISTS."
– MAHATMA GANDHI

Just like a steadfast lighthouse amidst a raging storm, casting its beacon to guide ships safely to harbor, "The Guiding Light," the fourth chapter of my journey, symbolizes an undying source of illumination on my path to a promising future - my grandmother.

As we delve into this segment of my journey, you will accompany me through my early years in America. You'll witness my efforts to navigate new cultural norms, my struggles with homesickness, and the challenges of an education system markedly different from what I knew.

But amidst these trials, there will also be moments of clarity and revelation, significantly marked by the guiding wisdom of my grandma. Her teachings emerged as my North Star, aiding me in navigating these unfamiliar waters. Her unwavering faith in me became my armor, and even in her passing, her influence persisted, continually shaping my decisions and fortifying my resolve to press on.

This chapter intertwines the bittersweet moments leading up to my wedding - a joyous occasion shadowed by the soul-deep pain of bidding farewell to my guiding light. The loss signified the end of an era and triggered a profound emotional earthquake that resonated deep within me.

"The Guiding Light" transcends mere chapters; it stands as a tribute to the enduring legacy of my grandmother, the formidable power of family bonds, and the love that transcends our physical existence. It serves as a threshold where the harsh winds of adversity yield to the soft glow of hope, where echoes of the past harmonize with the melodies of the future, orchestrating a symphony of resilience, determination, and the unwavering pursuit of a better life.

Through the narrative of this chapter, you'll witness how even in the darkest corners, a light can always find its way, guiding us toward our destiny. You'll see how loss can shape our purpose, compelling us to honor the memory of those we've loved by embodying their values and carrying forward their dreams. Together, let us unravel the profound impact of my grandma's love, her lessons, and the transformative power of grief, illuminating our path as we journey forward.

MEMORIES OF A RESILIENT WOMAN: MY GRANDMOTHER

Ma Kumba Saah Sakawolo, my grandmother, embodied extraordinary strength and resilience. A beacon of hope and the embodiment of selfless love, she hailed from the humble town of Foya in Lofa County, Liberia. This northeastern county was her home, where she laid the foundation of her legendary life.

Named after her town, Sakawolo, she wore this title like a badge of honor, carrying it with dignity and pride throughout her life. As a young girl, she was renowned for her hard work and profound respect for everyone. She was more than just a resident of Sakawolo; she was an integral part of its fabric. Her greatness was recognized not only in her birthplace but also by the echo of her name resonating far and wide, touching every heart privileged to know her.

If I were to narrate tales of her benevolence, words would fall short. Ma Kumba Saah Sakawolo was that remarkable woman who willingly offered her meal to a stranger, even if it meant her children would go hungry. Her spirit of sacrifice remained unwavering, a steady beacon amidst life's unpredictable tides. This selflessness, her innate instinct to prioritize others over herself, defined her character. It was her distinguishing feature, what truly made her Ma Kumba Saah Sakawolo.

Just as the resilient oak tree imparts its strength to its seedlings, my grandmother bestowed her virtues upon her children. Chief among them was my mother, who represented the values instilled by Ma Kumba. The wisdom she collected from her mother was not taught but absorbed, a product of years spent observing and admiring her. My mother became a reflection of my grandmother, a living testament to her upbringing and a tangible embodiment of her legacy.

When I reflect on the formidable women who have molded my life, my thoughts turn to my grandmother and my mother. They stand as towering figures of resilience and selflessness, their lives a testament to unwavering strength and steadfast commitment to their values.

My grandmother radiated a spirit of service, finding joy in extending kindness and support to others. Whether through her community cooking, assisting family and friends, or fulfilling her church duties, she dedicated herself wholeheartedly. Her unwavering commitment was evident in her active participation in the church choir for decades, a commitment that persisted until her final days. Looking back on the moments I spent with her in church as a child, I now realize the profound significance of her actions; she was sowing seeds of generosity and service that would blossom with time.

Her dedication to service extended far beyond our community to her involvement in her church choir, a pursuit she held dear to her heart. The recollection of her sharing a DVD of her choir's performance with us during her visit to the United States for my wedding remains vivid in my memory. Despite the language barrier, as the songs were in her native Kissi, the music stirred deep emotions, showcasing her steadfast commitment to utilizing her talents for the service of others and for God.

In a sense, her legacy of service has been bestowed upon me, as I now find myself deeply engaged in serving within my church community. I recognize that my intimate bond with my grandmother, being the grandchild who spent the most time with her, has significantly shaped my path. Living under the same roof in West Point and frequently accompanying her and my mother to the waterside general market during school breaks have left me with cherished memories that continue to influence me.

My teenage years were characterized by responsibilities that honed my resilience. Moving to live with my grandmother in New Georgia Estate marked the beginning of my involvement in household chores and her charcoal business. I took on early responsibilities such as overseeing the purchase and transportation of coal for her business. While these experiences were demanding, they played a pivotal role in shaping me for life's journey ahead.

Reflecting on my childhood, I recall often teasing my grandmother about her broken English, not fully understanding the generational and cultural gaps that influenced her life. Education, especially for women during her era, wasn't emphasized, leaving her with fewer opportunities compared to what I and my children have today. Despite my jests, her playful scoldings and her endearing nickname for me, "her small husband," were manifestations of her affection and humor, crafting cherished memories that I hold dear to this day.

An unforgettable moment occurred during her visit to the United States when she referred to me as her husband in front of my wife. This cultural nuance, puzzling to my wife, required an explanation, highlighting the profound cultural and familial ties that my grandmother and I shared.

My grandmother's life wasn't a path strewn with roses, nor was it a journey paved with privilege. Hers was a life of hardship, a relentless struggle against the odds. Yet, she stood resolute, unbowed, and unbroken. From a young girl born in a small Liberian town to becoming the very heartbeat of that community, she traversed a path far from easy. Throughout her journey, she never wavered in her values. With each step, she radiated selflessness like a guiding light, illuminating the path for others.

Similarly, my mother's life mirrored the teachings of her own mother. She was the embodiment of my grandmother's legacy, the culmination of her lifelong sacrifice and devotion. My mother embodied the lessons imparted by her mother, serving as a living testament to her teachings.

As I reflect on the past, I recognize that these two extraordinary women were not merely role models but the architects of my resilience. Their fortitude became my own, their teachings my guiding light. Their unwavering determination in the face of adversity fueled my perseverance and refusal to surrender. They instilled in me the value of resilience, teaching me to rise stronger from every setback.

Through the trials they faced, they epitomized resilience, imparting the lesson that true character is forged not in times of ease, but in adversity. I discovered that resilience isn't about avoiding life's blows, but about enduring them and pressing forward. These teachings have served as my beacon, guiding me through life's tempestuous waters.

In my grandmother, I witnessed a woman whose heart overflowed with boundless selflessness. Through my mother, I glimpsed a reflection of her mother's wisdom, a living embodiment of her enduring legacy. Both, through their lives and actions, imparted to me the essence of resilience. They taught me to stand unwavering amid adversity, to bend without breaking under pressure, and to persevere relentlessly. This is the legacy they bestowed upon me—the legacy of resilience. And this legacy is woven into the fabric of who I am today. Their indomitable spirit of resilience serves as my armor, shielding me in the face of life's trials, and I wear it with pride.

My beloved grandmother is on the left and my cherished mother is on the right.

THE HEARTACHE AND HEALING: CONFRONTING LOSS AND EMBRACING GRIEF

Her spirit lingered within the confines of our home, a familiar presence in the laughter of our children, a subtle murmur in the sway of the curtains, a silent solace in the stillness of our nights. I often found myself longing for her company, for the solace of her comforting words, for the warmth of her contagious laughter. Our home seemed incomplete without her, and the rift left by her absence was profound and all-encompassing.

I started a quest, a journey inside myself, to find and face my buried feelings. This looking inside made me think more about my memories, bringing back experiences that I hadn't thought about in a long time. I realized that I wasn't just sad because she wasn't here, but also because there were stories she didn't get to tell, wisdom she didn't share, and love she didn't express.

In my search for closure, I revisited the wonderful moments we shared, the lessons she taught me, and the values she ingrained in me. I journeyed back through memories, each step stirring a new feeling, each recollection a clear picture of my time with her.

My grandmother was a reservoir of wisdom and knowledge. Despite her lack of formal education and her often broken language, she possessed a remarkable gift for storytelling. Her narratives, brimming with wisdom, remain a beacon for me. Through tales of her tireless efforts to educate her children and provide for their basic needs despite countless challenges, she illuminated the complexities of life. She uncovered the resilience of the human spirit and the unwavering determination to thrive against all odds.

There were moments when despair loomed over me when the enormity of her absence felt overwhelming. In those times, I sought solace in my memories of her. I held onto her words, her wisdom lighting the way, leading me through the darkest corners of my grief.

I found solace in her teachings and the values, she had instilled in me. My grandmother had taught me the importance of resilience and the bravery to confront challenges directly. She believed in the resilience of the human spirit, in its remarkable ability to heal and rise again. It was this resilience, this inner strength, that carried me through the stormy waves of my grief.

As months turned into years, the raw pain of her departure began to fade, evolving into a scar—a touching reminder of my loss. Yet, with time, I came to understand that my grandmother had never truly departed. She resided within me, within the values she had embedded, the wisdom she had bestowed, and the love she had given.

Her passing imparted invaluable lessons about life, grief, and healing. It underscored the inevitability of loss, the universality of grief, and the astonishing resilience of the human spirit. It compelled me to confront my vulnerabilities, to recognize my pain, and to navigate through my sorrow. Through this journey, it paved the path toward healing, acceptance, and personal growth.

Today, as I stand at the threshold between the past and the present, I take comfort in the knowledge that my grandmother's essence persists within me. I pay tribute to her legacy by embracing her teachings, embodying her wisdom, and perpetuating her spirit of resilience. I endeavor to embody the man she envisioned me to be – compassionate, strong, and resilient. Her memory remains a source of inspiration, her teachings a guiding light, and her love a nurturing force in my life.

My journey through grief was a voyage of self-discovery, an expedition that laid the groundwork for healing and personal growth. It taught me the potency of vulnerability, the bravery of acceptance, and the resilience born from forgiveness. Through navigating the tumultuous waves of loss, I found solace in cherished memories of love, emerging from the ordeal more resilient and fortified than before.

As I write down these memoirs, I come to understand that my grandmother's influence transcends the realms of the living. Her spirit reverberates within me, her wisdom illuminates my journey, and her love enriches my existence. Though I yearn for her physical presence, her essence remains etched deeply within my soul. In life, she was my guiding light, and even in death, she continues to be my celestial beacon, guiding me through life's tumultuous voyage.

I treasured my grandmother's stories deeply. As a young boy, they offered me solace. These tales weren't mere narratives—they served as a portal to a past I hadn't lived, a link to my ancestors, our customs, and our collective family history. They imparted lessons of life, bravery, affection, resilience, and sagacity. Embedded within each story was a strand of unwavering love, the significance of community, and the necessity of remaining faithful to one's heritage.

Her stories sprang to life through her eyes, her voice rich with emotion, her gestures animated, and her laughter warm. She possessed a distinctive manner of storytelling, her voice weaving the rhythm of the tale, each nuance enhancing the depth of the narrative. With her words, she crafted vibrant pictures, breathing life into characters and enveloping us in the realms she conjured.

Now, as I ponder about her, I comprehend that she wasn't merely recounting tales; she was giving wisdom, transmitting the knowledge of our forebears, and knitting together the fabric of our culture and customs. Each story formed a thread in that tapestry, adding to a portrait as vivid as our heritage. It's these narratives, these recollections of her, that have supported me through my sorrow.

As I wrestled with her departure, I found solace in her stories. They provided me with a connection to her, a reassuring presence despite her absence. They recalled the times we spent together—the laughter, the happiness, the wisdom, and even the tears. Her stories became my haven, my sanctuary amidst the tempest of my sorrow.

Each story served as a testament to her indomitable spirit, her bravery, and her steadfast love for us. They served as a reminder of the values she instilled in us, values that still influence me today. As I contemplate her life and the influence, she had on me, I recognize the magnitude of her legacy. She persists in our memories, in the teachings she imparted, and in the affection, she bestowed upon us.

Her passing left a profound void in my life, an emptiness that no words could adequately express. Yet, amidst my grief, I've stumbled upon a route to healing. I've come to understand that grieving isn't a straightforward journey; rather, it's a winding path marked by peaks and valleys, ebbs and flows. There are instances of acute anguish and moments of tranquility. There are periods when the loss seems insurmountable, and times when memories offer solace.

Throughout this journey, I've embraced my grief, permitting myself to experience the sorrow, to shed tears, and to mourn. It's through this cathartic process that I've discovered healing. The pain hasn't vanished, but it's merged into my being, a testament to the affection I harbored for my grandmother—a love that transcends the realms of existence.

My voyage through grief and recovery follows a path that is both profoundly personal and universally human. Through losing my grandmother, I've attained a deeper insight into the human capability for love and sorrow. In mourning her passing, I've unearthed the influence of her life and the potency of her legacy. Though she's physically departed, her guidance endures, urging me to embrace life with love, fortitude, resilience, and optimism. For this, I am endlessly thankful.

In commemorating my grandmother, I aim to pay homage to her life, to commemorate her wisdom, and to perpetuate her legacy. Her lessons, values, and love have molded me into the individual I am today. They have steered me through my bleakest hours and illuminated my route toward recovery. Her essence endures, not solely within me, but in all those she has influenced. And through our shared recollections, she persists as a source of inspiration, guidance, and affection. Her life was a precious gift, a boon, a lesson. And even in her absence, her legacy shines brightly.

CELEBRATING THE MATRIARCH: AN EVERLASTING TRIBUTE

The bond I shared with my grandmother, Ma Kumba Saah Sakawolo, was unlike any other. It was a connection forged through time, enriched by shared moments, and reinforced by a profound love that surpassed generations. It seemed as though she possessed an innate radar that linked her to my heart, allowing her to perceive my joys, fears, dreams, and doubts. Her presence in my life resembled a gentle, reassuring blanket, offering warmth and shelter from life's harsh realities.

One of my dearest aspirations was to witness my grandmother cradling my first child in her arms, her weathered fingers tenderly tracing his tiny features, her eyes filled with the same joy and hope mirrored in mine. It was a dream I held close, a vision that depicted happiness and the bond between generations. Yet, fate had woven a different narrative.

My wife and I eagerly awaited the arrival of our first child, envisioning a future brimming with laughter, love, and endless happiness. However, our hopes were dashed when my wife encountered complications during her pregnancy, resulting in the heartbreaking loss of our son, born prematurely at eighteen weeks. The world came to a standstill around us, enveloped in a profound silence echoing with the reverberations of our sorrow. I found myself engulfed in a turbulent sea of grief, longing for the comforting presence of my grandmother, her reassuring words, and the solace of her embrace.

How I longed for her presence, a source of comfort in the painful void left by our loss. I yearned for her wisdom, her soothing words, her reassuring presence. I yearned to share my journey with her, to witness the pride in her eyes as I revealed the chapters of the man I have become.

Her story, and in essence, our story together, stands as a testament to her indomitable spirit, her unwavering resilience. She was the unseen force that guided me, the invisible wind beneath my wings, urging me to reach for my aspirations. Her teachings have acted as my compass, steering me towards the route of bravery, perseverance, and accomplishment.

Her essence is woven into every step I take, in every obstacle I face. She was the steadfast pillar that upheld our family, the guiding light that led us through life's turbulent trials. Her values are etched deeply within me, molding my character and forming the foundation upon which I've constructed my life.

Every triumph I've attained, every obstacle I've overcome, is a tribute to her, a tribute to her enduring spirit and unwavering belief in me. The lessons she taught me continue to steer me, and her boundless love strengthens me. Even though she's no longer with us, she remains a wellspring of inspiration, her legacy residing within me, motivating me to pursue excellence, to remain resilient in the face of adversity, and to never yield to challenges. Her memory is a cherished keepsake, a guiding light that brightens my path during life's darkest hours. Our shared narrative, her narrative, stands as a testament to the resilient human spirit, the spirit of fortitude that she instilled in me. It's a legacy of love, wisdom, and resilience that I carry onward.

As time passed, I discovered comfort in her teachings and resilience in her wisdom. Her words reverberated in my thoughts, providing direction in my voyage. Though she couldn't hold my son or partake in the joy of new life, I sensed her presence in every instant, every heartbeat. She existed within the love I hold for my wife, within the courage to confront our loss, within the resolve to construct a future filled with hope.

Through the disturbance of our loss, my wife and I have emerged resilient. We've acquired the skill to navigate the turbulent waves of grief, to discover comfort in our mutual love, and to find optimism in the prospect of tomorrow. My grandmother's fortitude, her resilience, her steadfast trust in life's benevolence, has transformed into our guiding light, steering us through the tempest towards a future illuminated with hope, fortitude, and affection. Throughout this odyssey, we've learned that even in loss, there lies gain. Amidst agony, there blooms growth. And even in death, love persists.

So, even as my heart grieves the loss of my grandmother and mourns the tragic end of my son's budding life, I've discovered solace in their memories. I've gathered strength from my grandmother's sagacity, mustered the bravery to confront life's challenges, and clung to the unwavering hope for a brighter tomorrow. Their memories have intertwined with my being, shaping my narrative—a tale of resilience, love, and an everlasting spirit. It's a narrative I'll carry forth, a legacy that shall endure. And in this manner, they persist, their spirits guiding, inspiring, and loving me. They are the force propelling me onward, urging me to ascend higher, to reach further, and to live a life imbued with purpose, love, and resilience. For this, I am infinitely grateful.

In the months following the loss of our first child, the world underwent a transformation that felt both sudden and surreal. The tone of our son's fleeting existence echoed through the quietness of our home, saturating every space with a intense ache. The walls bore silent testimony to our isolated sorrow, to the ghostly cries of an infant who would never experience the love of his parents, his grandparents. His room, meticulously arranged with anticipation and delight, now stood eerily vacant—a poignant reminder of a life that might have been, a life that ought to have been.

It was during this period of unfathomable grief that I came to fully grasp the profundity of my grandmother's wisdom, the depth of her teachings. Her resilience wasn't merely about weathering the storms; it was about discovering the rhythm in the rain, finding delight in the most modest of joys, cherishing every moment, every breath, every heartbeat. It was about embracing the anguish, yet refusing to let it shape our identity. It was about standing steadfast amidst the wreckage, transmuting it into milestones towards a brighter, sturdier, more resilient future.

Even in her absence, my grandmother remained my beacon of hope, illuminating my path through the darkest of times. Her memory became my sanctuary, her teachings my guiding star. She existed within me, a vital part of my being. In my struggles, in my triumphs, in my resilience, I glimpsed echoes of her indomitable spirit, her unwavering bravery, her unyielding resilience. Throughout my journey of healing and acceptance, my grandmother's teachings stood by me as steadfast companions, her memory a wellspring of inspiration.

Though I couldn't introduce her to my son, I pledged to raise him in her honor, imparting to him the cherished values she embodied. His legacy would be entwined with hers, a tribute to the woman who, though unable to cradle him in her arms, cherished him deeply in her heart. The essence of Ma Kumba Saah Sakawolo would endure through him, through his experiences, and his narrative. It would be a tale of love, loss, resilience, and hope—the tale of an indomitable human spirit, the tale of our bond.

My beloved late grandmother, Ma Kumba Saah Sakawolo during one of her shopping trips in the United States.

The Power of Transformation

Transformation is born from challenge. In this chapter, my journey from rebellion to realization unfolds, guided by discipline and the pursuit of knowledge. It illustrates the pivotal moments of my metamorphosis, highlighting the crucial role of education and community.

5

Turning Pages

"THE BEST WAY TO PREDICT THE FUTURE IS TO CREATE IT." – ABRAHAM LINCOLN

As we turn the pages of our lives, every chapter unfolds a new narrative, a new opportunity for transformation. In the fifth chapter, "Turning Pages," we find ourselves at the precipice of such a transformative journey.

Moving to America marked a monumental shift, signifying more than mere geographic relocation. It symbolized transformation. Here, I embarked on a journey of reevaluating my outlooks, reshaping my mindsets, and redefining my identity—flipping not only the pages in my narrative but also the chapters in my life.

With every page I turned, I showcased my resilience and dedication to evolve, propelled by an unwavering aspiration for a brighter future. From academic challenges to cultural adjustments, every obstacle served as a chance for personal development. Each page turned marked a stride towards grasping the true essence of my identity and charting the course toward the person I aspired to be.

"Turning Pages" embodies more than just external shifts in my environment or circumstances; it captures internal transformation. It signifies the transition from despair to hope, from helplessness to empowerment, and from being a bystander to an engaged author in shaping my life narrative.

This chapter unveils the tale of my metamorphosis amidst adversity. It delves into the ability to reshape one's story amid challenges, the power of human resilience, and the bravery to persevere, adapt, and grow.

As we journey through "Turning Pages," you'll witness a voyage of self-discovery and transformation, illustrating that our response to challenges, not the challenges themselves, defines us. Join me as we explore this transformative odyssey, one page at a time.

MY FAITH AS ANCHOR: DISCOVERING PURPOSE AND COMMUNITY IN SERVICE

Over time, my connection to the church community strengthened, becoming a vital part of my life. What began as modest volunteering, initially helping out with the choir's Saturday performances, evolved into a diverse journey of service. I discovered my niche within the church's audio department, a role that resonated deeply with me and offered a distinctive means of contributing to our gatherings. This initial involvement served as a springboard for embracing additional responsibilities with enthusiasm and open arms.

A pivotal moment in my journey arose when my wife, not just my life partner but also my guiding light in church service, needed to scale back her commitments due to the demands of our growing family following the arrival of our first son. It was then that I found myself assuming additional roles, including duties in the administrative office—a responsibility I not only embraced but flourished in. The church became my central focus, a refuge shielding me from the distractions and temptations that often ensnare young people. Amidst the tumult of adolescence and early adulthood, when many of my peers strayed off course, the guidance, prayers, and fellowship within the church anchored me, keeping me resolute in my principles and objectives.

The layers of my dedication to service weren't solely crafted during my time in the United States; they had roots that stretched back to my days in Liberia, where my involvement with the church was equally fervent. During that time, I embraced various roles, ranging from the humility of cleaning to the weight of teaching Sunday School. My engagement took a significant turn when the pastor, who had welcomed me into this spiritual family, departed unexpectedly. In the void of leadership that followed, I found myself, somewhat unintentionally, stepping forward to guide our small congregation through the interim period. It was a testament to my commitment and, perhaps, to the faith the community vested in me. Despite being one of the youngest members, I carried the responsibility with a sense of duty and purpose, ensuring the continuity of our gatherings until a new shepherd could be found.

This small church, humble in size yet profound in its influence on my life, eventually ceased its operations. The congregation dispersed, with many finding new spiritual homes in larger branches or alternative churches. This chapter concluded shortly before I relocated to reside with my late grandmother in New Georgia, Liberia—a transition that signaled another pivotal juncture in my life's trajectory.

Reflecting on these experiences, it's evident that the essence of service has been a consistent thread woven into the tapestry of my life, a principle deeply rooted in me by my family's legacy. "Service is the rent we pay for being. It is the very purpose of life, and not something you do in your spare time," as Marian Wright Edelman so eloquently articulated. This quote resonates with my journey, highlighting the inherent value of service as a fundamental aspect of my identity. The spirit of service was transmitted to me by my parents and, most notably, my grandmother. Both my mother and grandmother actively served in their church, lending their voices to the choir, while my father devoted his time as an usher. This familial tradition of service profoundly shaped my approach to life, instilling in me a deep sense of responsibility and community involvement.

In line with this, the Bible offers a scripture that has always guided my path: *"For even the Son of Man did not come to be served, but to serve, and to give His life as a ransom for many" (Mark 10:45).* This verse summarizes the principles of my service, reminding me that the greatest fulfillment comes not from being served, but from serving others. It reflects a legacy of commitment and faith that transcends geographical borders and life stages, shaping me into the individual I am today.

Through this odyssey of service, spanning both my time in Liberia and my present involvement in the church community, I've gleaned that giving back transcends mere roles; it's about the hearts we uplift and the lives we enrich—including our own. Service, as exemplified by my family, is life's noble calling, enriching the spirit and fostering unity among communities with a shared purpose. My experiences, nurtured by the teachings of my parents and illuminated by scripture, persist in steering me along a journey of purposeful engagement and spiritual contentment.

Sharing this chapter of my narrative is more than recounting my journey; it's a testimony to my faith. My mother and grandmother, towering figures of strength and resilience in my life, prayed for me ceaselessly. Observing their unwavering faith and resilience during my formative years instilled within me a profound belief in and dedication to my faith. This belief serves as a driving force, imparting strength, offering solace, and guiding me as I traverse the complexities of life in a foreign land.

The echoes of their prayers, their steadfast faith, and their unwavering strength continue to touch me to this day, offering comfort and direction as I navigate the maze of life in a foreign land. Throughout this journey, I've discovered the importance of clinging to my faith, and anchoring myself to my spiritual beliefs, no matter the storms that may arise.

I carry the lessons of my homeland, my family, and my faith with me always. They have shaped me and continue to influence my journey. I am a product of my past, the son of resilient parents, a bearer of a powerful legacy, and a believer in a faith that holds me steady in the storm. My journey from Liberia to the United States is one of faith, resilience, and unwavering hope. And I continue to navigate this path, armed with the blessings of my parents, the prayers of my grandmother, and the unwavering belief in a power higher than us all.

The journey has been a complex tapestry of experiences, a blend of the joyous and the heart-wrenching. Yet, every thread in this tapestry, every twist and turn of my journey, has molded me into who I am today. And for this, I am eternally grateful. The legacy of my faith, the resilience of my family, and the memories of my homeland continue to inspire me, pushing me forward, helping me soar to greater heights. I hope my story serves as a testament to the power of faith, resilience, and the unbreakable human spirit.

And so, I walk this path, taking each day as it comes, driven by my faith, sustained by the love and lessons of my family, and guided by the memories of my homeland. I hold on to the belief that, no matter the challenges life throws my way, the faith instilled in me by my mother and grandmother was not merely a crutch for getting through the tough times. It was also a moral compass that guided me, a source of comfort during the dark days, and a beacon of hope for brighter tomorrows. Their daily prayers didn't just echo in the corners of our Liberian home; they reverberated in my heart, and it was these prayers that often became the soundtrack to my dreams in this new country.

Every Sunday, we would gather at Christ the King Miracle Church, Tulsa, a sanctuary from the struggles of daily life and a fortress for our faith. The powerful praise and worship, the prayers, the inspirational and uplifting sermon - it all became familiar, a melody of solace that helped us adjust to our new surroundings.

The sense of community at the church was profound, mirroring the communal spirit we had left behind in Liberia on the Rock. I found a new family in the form of older men and women who became my surrogate uncles and aunts. These individuals stepped in to guide me and provide wisdom when I needed it most, becoming a pivotal part of my upbringing in America.

My dedication to the church extended beyond my spiritual growth. It also offered me a chance to contribute to our community. I assisted with choir presentations on Saturdays, and soon, serving became second nature to me, a regular part of my routine. Church service wasn't just about commitment; it was a labor of love and a testament to my faith.

The church was also where I met the love of my life, my wife. She wasn't the reason I started volunteering, but our paths crossed in that sacred space, weaving our lives together most beautifully.

Navigating the unfamiliar terrain of American high school, I found myself disadvantaged due to my background and prior experiences. The educational system in Liberia differed greatly from what I encountered in the United States. Despite my initial setback, I embraced the challenge, keeping my eyes fixed on the broader goal. Education, I realized, was my key to success, my means of ascending the ladder to the elusive American Dream.

The transition was challenging, but I remained undeterred. Attending school during the weekdays with assignments and chores, coupled with working on the weekends, initially appeared as daunting mountains. Yet, akin to scaling a peak, I realized it would demand endurance, effort, and perseverance. Confronting my fears, overcoming insecurities, and pushing my limits became imperative, fueled by the understanding that the view from the summit would justify the climb.

Eventually, my parents secured a larger apartment where we could all reside together. This relocation not only enabled me to attend school within the district, diminishing my commute and affording me more study time, but it also brought about a significant shift. It wasn't solely about the proximity to school; it was about uniting under one roof as a family, sharing our lives, dreams, and challenges.

This journey to the United States transcended mere geography; it was a journey of profound transformation. It entailed shedding old identities and embracing new ones, preserving cherished traditions while immersing in unfamiliar cultures, enduring hardships while nurturing hopes. Throughout, I clung to my roots, values, and faith, honoring the invaluable lessons passed down by my grandmother and mother, who epitomized resilience. Their prayers resonated in my heart, their teachings echoed in my mind, and their love enveloped my soul. I am, and forever will be, a product of their strength, wisdom, and resilience. Through this memoir, I not only share my narrative but also theirs. They sculpted my spirit, instilling in me the courage to transcend adversities, to persist in the face of challenges, and to hold steadfast to the belief in miracles.

PURSUING THE AMERICAN DREAM

In my early experiences in America, working at Taco Bell wasn't just a job; it was a crucial part of my journey toward the American Dream. I had just arrived from Liberia at 17, and within the hustle and bustle of this fast-food environment—amidst sizzling tacos and the constant rush of the drive-thru—I faced and conquered many challenges. These experiences tested my determination, honed my skills, and profoundly influenced the course of my life.

The journey began with a mix of excitement and apprehension. Accompanied by my mother and aunt, I recall feeling the weight of uncertainty as I entered the restaurant to submit my application. My accent, a proud reflection of my Liberian heritage, proved to be a significant communication barrier. Despite my proficiency in English, this difference often led to frustration and even hostility from customers. Instances where customers demanded assistance from someone else or rudely told me to "go back to Africa" were especially disheartening. However, in those moments of rejection and hurt, I discovered an inner strength, choosing to not take it personally but to press on.

Amidst these challenges, Mrs. Donna, my manager, emerged as a pillar of support. Recognizing my capabilities, she gradually entrusted me with a wide range of responsibilities. My duties at Taco Bell were varied and educational, ranging from dishwashing and cleaning the lobby to food preparation and managing the drive-thru. This array of tasks offered me a special chance to learn, grow, and affirm my value. My hard work did not go unnoticed, ultimately leading to my promotion to shift manager upon my high school graduation.

The strangeness of American culture, like the bustling late-night service at Taco Bell, initially puzzled me. Yet, these experiences provided a distinctive perspective for me to comprehend and appreciate my new home. The late hours, the diverse range of customers, and the multitude of tasks as a shift manager all contributed to my increasing familiarity with American life and work ethics.

After enduring a taxing shift at Taco Bell, I frequently found solace in the steady rhythm of pedaling my bike through the quiet streets of the American suburbs. Despite my physical weariness, these nighttime bike rides evolved into a meditative practice, providing me with precious moments of reflection. The crisp night air against my skin, the shimmering stars overhead, and the peaceful hum of the world around me all worked together to calm my spirit, offering a refreshing counterpoint to the hustle and bustle of the fast-food environment.

This duality in my life was striking. In the midst of the flurry of orders and the chaos of the kitchen, I was merely a cog in the expansive machinery of capitalism, completely absorbed in the American hustle. Yet, as I pedaled through the night, time appeared to slow down. The noise faded into a serene quietness, and the frantic rush was replaced by tranquility. It was in these reflective moments that I could fully grasp the magnitude of my journey—from the comforting familiarity of Liberia to the ambitious, sometimes harsh landscapes of the United States.

However, on one particular night, my ride took an unexpected twist. The sky, once clear, swiftly turned gloomy as clouds gathered into thick formations. What started as a light sprinkle soon escalated into a torrential downpour, drenching my clothes and sending a chill deep into my bones. Beyond the physical discomfort, the rain mirrored the turmoil of my struggles—the uncertainty of my circumstances, the longing for home, and the relentless grind of work and study. Each raindrop that poured on my face felt like an questioning of my dreams, my decisions, and my pursuit of the elusive American dream.

Yet, despite the cold and discomfort, I stumbled upon an unexpected solace in the rain. It acted as a purifier, cleansing away the dirt of everyday existence and freeing me from my worries and apprehensions. Though the rain was unforgiving, it carried a therapeutic quality. It was nature's way of testing my resilience, questioning my resolve. In turn, I welcomed it, acknowledged the challenge, and pushed through the storm with determination.

The journey home that night went beyond just navigating through a storm; it captured the essence of my life's journey, filled with trials and aspirations. The rain, the cold, and the exhaustion were intrinsic to my pursuit of the American dream, symbolizing the obstacles that would strengthen me, strengthening my resilience along the way.

The journey was grueling, but it was also incredibly fulfilling. Every pedal push, every mile covered, every raindrop weathered served as a testament to my determination and perseverance. It represented the promise I had made to myself and to my family back in Liberia, a vow to strive, to thrive, and to seize every opportunity presented by this new land.

Upon arriving home, the storm had subsided. Drenched and shivering, yet my spirit burned brightly, undiminished. I stood firm, infused with a deep sense of achievement. I had braved the storm, both literal and metaphorical, and emerged victorious. I had faced the challenges of my journey head-on and had prevailed.

That night, amidst the downpour, I gained deep insights into my American dream—insights that no book or lecture could provide. The dream wasn't just about material wealth or achievement; it was about resilience, grit, and perseverance. It meant facing the storms head-on, turning challenges into opportunities, and emerging stronger on the other side. In the midst of that storm, soaked to the bone and chilled to the core, I grasped a profound understanding of the American dream. It wasn't merely a destination; it was a journey—a journey marked by trials, hardships, and victories—a journey to which I was wholeheartedly committed, regardless of the weather.

The daily demands at Taco Bell went beyond just an initiation into the American workforce; they embodied an unexpected journey of personal development and resilience. The bustling environment of the fast-food chain sharply contrasted with the academic tranquility I was accustomed to. In this new realm, the intensity of the fryer's heat, the rapidity of one's hands, and the precision of movements dictated the rhythm of the day. It was a world of relentless peak hours, forced smiles, and taxing tasks that demanded my full focus and effort.

Despite the demanding nature of the job, a camaraderie flourished among my coworkers and me—a diverse group of individuals, each with our own stories and dreams. Bound by shared experiences, mutual respect, and shared goals, we evolved beyond mere colleagues; we became fellow dreamers, navigating our distinct paths in this expansive land of opportunities.

In those fleeting moments of tranquility, when the rush of customers subsided, I found myself lost in introspection. While occupied with tasks like cleaning counters, restocking shelves, and mopping floors, I reflected on the intricate path that had brought me to that precise moment. The dreams that had ignited my journey, although now appearing distant and somewhat obscured by the reality of my daily life, continued to serve as a guiding light, navigating me through the trials and tribulations.

Concurrently with my time at Taco Bell, I embarked on an academic journey at Tulsa Community College (TCC), initially spurred by my family's encouragement toward nursing. Mrs. Donna, always supportive, graciously accommodated my academic commitments, nurturing my aspirations with steadfast encouragement. However, as I immersed myself in the medical field through nursing assistant training, I experienced a pivotal revelation: my true calling lay in a different direction. The moment I disclosed my decision to leave Taco Bell and pursue further education was fraught with emotion. Mrs. Donna, who had become a maternal figure to me, along with colleagues who felt like family, shared in my bittersweet transition, expressing both sadness at my departure and unwavering support for my future endeavors.

My departure from Taco Bell was marked by a memorable Christmas party, a heartfelt tribute to our shared journey and the profound connections we had formed. Joined by a friend who would later become my wife and lifelong companion, I brought a taste of Liberia to the celebration through my mother's cooking, sharing our culture and stories with my Taco Bell family.

Looking back on my time at Taco Bell, I see it not just as a job, but as a transformative experience teeming with lessons in resilience, flexibility, and pursuing dreams. This chapter, brimming with challenges and personal development, played a vital role in readying me for what lay ahead, reinforcing the notion that every encounter, no matter how seemingly insignificant, adds depth to our life's voyage, molding us into our ultimate selves.

During this period, I found myself constantly balancing the demands of work at Taco Bell and my academic pursuits. Despite the demanding atmosphere of the fast-food chain, my dedication to education remained steadfast, propelling me toward a brighter tomorrow. Balancing these dual commitments extended my days, blending them into a seamless cycle from sunrise to sunset. However, instead of overwhelming me, this demanding schedule ignited my determination to succeed and to craft a life that reflected my aspirations.

The journey home from work, frequently navigating through unpredictable weather and tiring bike rides, introduced further complexity to my path. Yet, I began to perceive these challenges not as hindrances, but as opportunities for personal growth, fortifying my resolve and laying the groundwork for even greater accomplishments.

That night, as I was beaten by the rain, I experienced an overwhelming sense of triumph, despite being drenched and chilled to the bone. The storm served as an emotional metaphor for my journey, encapsulating the obstacles, uncertainties, and hardships I encountered. However, persevering through the downpour, I tapped into a reservoir of strength within myself that I hadn't realized existed.

This epiphany illuminated that the pursuit of the American Dream was about more than simply reaching a destination; it was about the journey itself—the wisdom gained, the connections forged, and the personal growth experienced along the way. My narrative wasn't merely that of a Liberian teenager navigating a foreign land, but rather a testament to persistence, bravery, and the unwavering pursuit of one's dreams.

As I reflect on that pivotal chapter of my life today, I realize that my American Dream was never solely about financial prosperity or material possessions. It embraced the entire journey—the growth, the challenges, and the resilience encountered along the way. It was about persevering in the face of adversity, clinging to dreams even when they appeared distant, and discovering inner strength amid life's trials.

That phase of my life, marked by relentless work hours, a challenging academic regimen, and countless rain-soaked bike rides, surpassed mere hardship. It was a profound education, a guiding beacon, and a testament to the heart of the American Dream. Reflecting on my journey, I've realized that the dream isn't just a goal to reach; it's a voyage to embrace—a journey of personal evolution, a journey of striving to become the finest version of oneself. This,

I am convinced, encapsulates the genuine essence of the American Dream.

THE AMERICAN DREAM: A REALITY CHECK

My life appeared to be woven from the threads of challenge and resilience, struggle and victory. Each day, I navigated a tightrope, juggling the demanding responsibilities of a healthcare professional on one side and the pressing duties of a student on the other. It often felt like I was leading a dual existence, perpetually oscillating between these two worlds—distinct yet interconnected.

Every morning, I would greet the rising sun and make my way to school, my thoughts filled with the knowledge I aimed to gain and the dreams I was resolute to achieve. The endless lectures, daunting assignments, and unwavering pursuit of knowledge formed the foundation of my future, my American Dream. By nightfall, I would immerse myself in the realm of healthcare, where I not only witnessed the fragility of human life but also the remarkable resilience of the human spirit.

Amidst the weight of responsibilities and the wearisome routine, I discovered solace in my spiritual journey. The church emerged as my sanctuary, a refuge where I could escape the cacophony of the world and heed the gentle whispers of my soul. It wasn't merely a place of worship but also a beacon of community—a fragment of Liberia nestled in the heart of America. The familiar cadence of the hymns, the reassuring cadence of the sermons, and the shared laughter and stories wove together a blanket of familiarity, offering a taste of home in a foreign land.

Within the hallowed confines of the church, I encountered Pheona, a woman who personified grace, intellect, and compassion. Our mutual dedication to serving in the church forged a bond between us.

As weeks melted into months and months into years, I witnessed my purpose evolving, transcending the mere pursuit of survival

THE UNBREAKABLE HUMAN SPIRIT OF RESILIENCE

and individual accomplishments. It became more than obtaining a degree or securing a job; it transformed into a commitment to serve the community, effect change, and provide healing and aid to those in need. Working in the hospital, I bore witness to the cyclical nature of life and death, the fragility of human existence, and the remarkable resilience of the human spirit—and in those moments, I was deeply humbled.

But this sobering realization was not easily attained. There were days when I felt like a ship trapped in a storm, stricken by the ceaseless waves of obligations, fighting to stay above water. Frequently, I found myself embroiled in a tug-of-war—juggling my studies, my job, my personal life, and other commitments. I was constantly being pulled in disparate directions, each vying for my time, energy, and attention.

Yet, whenever I felt the weight of the overwhelming pressure threatening to engulf me, I would pause and reflect on how far I had journeyed. The boy who had once borne witness to the horrors of war, who had traversed the Atlantic Ocean with naught but a flicker of hope, who had arrived in a foreign land with dreams aglow in his eyes—he had endured, he had flourished. That boy was me, and I had traveled a considerable distance.

The voices of my family, both here in America and back home, served as a relief to my weary soul. Every call, every message, and every word they uttered infused me with a renewed sense of purpose and vitality to push forward. Their resilience, their unwavering belief in me, and their steadfast support acted as my lifeline, rescuing me from my darkest moments.

I won't deny that there were moments of despair, times when I questioned the validity of the American Dream. Yet, I would remind myself that dreams aren't handed to us on a silver platter. They necessitate sacrifice, demand persistence, and challenge our courage. I would gaze at my hands, weathered and hardened from the demanding labor, and discover hope. They stood as a testament to my journey, a symbol of my trials, and a pledge of my future.

In retrospect, every obstacle I encountered and conquered paved the way for the person I am today. Each setback was a chance for personal development, a lesson in fortitude. My journey was far from easy, but every drop of sweat, every tear shed, every sleepless night was worth it. The American Dream pulsed within me, as vibrant and powerful as ever. The horizon appeared closer than ever, and the sky seemed limitless.

As I immersed myself further in my studies, I discovered a renewed drive to excel, dedicating longer hours to my work at the hospital while managing my responsibilities with increased vigor. The hospital ceased to be merely a workplace; it transformed into a hub of learning and personal development. I actively engaged with the medical staff, seeking their guidance, learning from their experiences, and absorbing their wealth of knowledge.

At Saint Francis Hospital, I served as a nurse assistant, tending to the needs of patients. While some nights passed calmness, others were filled with the incessant beeping of bed alarms, signaling the distress of elderly and confused patients who occasionally failed to call for assistance, even those fully aware of their surroundings. It was a role suited not for the faint-hearted but for those willing to weather the relentless demands of the job—constantly changing, cleaning, and bathing patients, particularly those confined to their beds or struggling with confusion.

I vividly recall a particular night when I endeavored to care for a male patient who adamantly refused my assistance solely because of my race as a black man. This patient insisted on being attended to by someone of white descent and went as far as to hurl insults at me. I felt a profound sense of hurt and confusion, grappling with why someone who is seriously ill and need assistance would reject care based solely on race. Nevertheless, I chose not to take it personally and continued tending to other patients with diligence. To my surprise, the same patient later approached me at the end of the shift and offered a heartfelt apology, acknowledging that his behavior was unwarranted and unkind. He commended me for my kindness and compassion, expressing remorse for his earlier actions. I accepted his apology graciously, assuring him that I harbored no ill feelings. The hushed conversations among the medical staff and the physical tension in the air conveyed a narrative of resilience, hope, despair, and miracles.

During one eventful night, a colleague enlightened me about the Respiratory Therapy program at TCC. The notion struck a chord within me. It seemed like a trajectory that blended with my desire to serve, to alleviate pain, and to effect change. However, as I ventured down this avenue, a worrying sense of uncertainty started to take hold. Was this genuinely my calling? Was this the path preordained for me? With each step forward, the path grew increasingly fuzzy.

The nursing profession, renowned for its demanding responsibilities and critical role in healthcare, was one I held in utmost regard but ultimately did not envision for myself. I held nurses in high esteem for their unwavering commitment, resilience, and compassion. Nevertheless, I embarked on a quest for a different vocation—one that would infuse my life with a unique sense of purpose. While I harbored a strong desire to assist others, the specific path or career field through which I sought to make a difference remained elusive. What I was certain of, however, was that nursing, despite its noble pursuits, did not align with the path I envisioned for my future.

The uncertainty surrounding my career path weighed heavily on me each day. It loomed over my thoughts, casting a shadow over my perception of the world. This continuous thought cut away my peace of mind, yet my faith, my trust in God's plan, served as my sanctuary. I clung to the belief that every trial was a step toward the path meant for me. I had faith that my journey, though fraught with struggle, was not without purpose but rather a guiding force leading me toward my ultimate destiny.

Amidst the whirlwind of uncertainty, another facet of my life began to blossom—my relationship with Pheona. What started when I began volunteering at the church evolved into intimate conversations where we exchanged our dreams, aspirations, and anxieties. We sought solace in our shared experiences, both of us navigating this unfamiliar world far from our homelands. Her companionship became my sanctuary, her laughter a source of comfort. Like a pillar of strength, she mirrored the resilience and determination embodied by my mother and grandmother. Her unwavering faith in me and steadfast support infused a new depth into my journey.

In 2012, Pheona and I decided to elevate our relationship to the next level. As I knelt before her, presenting a ring, the world seemed to freeze in time. In that singular moment, all my doubts and worries faded away. Her eyes gleamed with love and affirmation, and I realized then that our future, our shared future, was brightly illuminated. Our engagement symbolized not only a commitment to love and companionship but also a fusion of our dreams and aspirations. We vowed to stand united through life's trials, to traverse the turbulent seas together, and to pursue our American Dream with unwavering determination.

Four years into our marriage, a newfound sense of clarity began to crystallize within me. I came to the profound realization that my true calling extended beyond the realms of diagnosing illnesses or treating physical maladies. My journey had illuminated the understanding that my purpose was to heal, to comfort, and to forge connections that transcended the physical realm. This profound insight served as the bedrock of my future career trajectory. I embarked on a quest for a profession that would enable me to nurture human connections, assuage emotional anguish, and empower individuals to pursue lives of fulfillment. It was during this period that I stumbled upon the field of psychology.

The science of understanding the human mind, delving into its depths to understand fears, hopes, and dreams, and facilitating healing and growth, felt like a calling that had been signaling me all along. Immersing myself in the literature of the field, I could envision myself in the role of a counselor or therapist, creating a nurturing environment for individuals to unravel their thoughts, confront their fears, and embark on a journey of self-discovery and development. I envisioned myself as a beacon of hope, a guiding light, illuminating the path for those grappling with the shadows of their struggles.

This realization ushered in a newfound peace and clarity. It felt as though a burdensome weight had been lifted from my shoulders, replaced by a light sense of purpose and a crystal-clear vision of the road ahead. The American Dream, once shrouded in uncertainty and fraught with challenges, now seemed within reach. I came to comprehend that my journey, full with its trials and tribulations, was not a hindrance but rather a springboard propelling me toward the realization of this dream.

With this newfound clarity, the horizon no longer appeared as distant as it once did. I could discern the skyline, shining with the golden light of dawn, proclaiming a day abundant with prospects, evolution, and triumph. In that moment, I harbored an unwavering conviction that my American Dream transcended mere survival and material success. It was about effecting change, about leaving an lasting mark, and about mending fractured hearts.

LOVE AND LOSS

In the heart of St. Francis Hospital, nestled amidst a jumble of corridors, the constant hum of medical machinery, and the hurried shuffle of healthcare practitioners, I found myself standing at a crossroads of pivotal life choices. I was entrenched within the trenches of the American healthcare system, steadfastly navigating the frontline, grappling with fatigue, juggling my professional obligations, and academic pursuits. I was akin to a soldier amidst the battlefield of existence, yet amidst the chaos, my family and my support, Pheona— the woman whose unwavering love served as my anchor, and who was soon to become my wife.

Pheona, a paragon of grace and resilience, served as a reflection of my journey and aspirations. She not only embraced my past but also shared my dreams, strengthening my hopes for the future. Our relationship stood as a testament to the strength of respect, mutual understanding, shared dreams, and collective struggles. Amidst the chaos of our bustling world, amidst the relentless grind of work and study, I found a fleeting moment of tranquility—a moment that felt ripe to invite her to intertwine her life with mine for eternity.

When she uttered the word 'Yes', the turbulent world around us, fraught with responsibilities and challenges, seemed to come to a standstill. It was as if time itself had paused to savor this joyous milestone in our lives. Happiness overflowed our hearts, radiating from our eyes and echoing in the smiles of our friends, families, and the cherished members of our church community—who had now become our extended family. In the summer of 2013, hand in hand, we strolled down the aisle, standing before God and our loved ones, pledging to navigate life's tempests together. Our love was consecrated amidst a symphony of joyous amens and heartfelt prayers.

Our love story, a testament to resilience and faith, was not immune to the ebb and flow of life's tides. We received the news that we were to become parents—a revelation that painted vibrant pictures of a future filled with the soft cooing of a newborn, the innocent laughter of a child, and the patter of tiny feet. We wove dreams around our firstborn, a son we affectionately named Desmond Junior, DJ. Our hearts brimmed with anticipation, and our home echoed with the promise of boundless laughter and unbridled joy.

But life, akin to a river, often carves its course, indifferent to the carefully laid plans on its banks. At eighteen weeks into the pregnancy, we suffered the devastating loss of DJ. It felt as though a bolt of lightning had cleaved through our dreams, scattering them into a myriad of shattered fragments. Our hearts, once brimming with excitement and joy, now bore the weight of a loss too profound to comprehend. Our home, once alive with the anticipation of DJ's arrival, now reverberated with a haunting silence.

Our journey towards parenthood took a heart-wrenching turn. Our arms, yearning to cradle our child, now hung heavy with emptiness. The nursery, lovingly prepared with anticipation, stood as a silent testament to the life we had lost too soon. Yet, amidst this tempest of despair, we discovered that we were not alone. Our friends, church community, and family enveloped us in a cocoon of support amidst the ocean of our grief. They were our steadfast anchors, catching us when we stumbled, lifting us when we fell, and providing refuge when the tempest of our loss threatened to overwhelm us.

In the absence left by DJ's departure, they inundated our lives with warmth, love, and unwavering faith. They enveloped us in their embrace, serving as constant reminders that we were not traversing this journey alone. Their silent solidarity acted as a soothing balm on our raw wounds. While the heartbreak initially felt insurmountable, it gradually began to wane—not because the pain diminished, but because we learned to bear it collectively.

The memory of DJ became interwoven with the very essence of our being, a cherished thread in the tapestry of our existence. We allowed our grief to flow freely—not as a symbol of surrender, but as a tribute to the boundless love we held for our unborn child. Clinging to each other, we reminded ourselves that this was merely a detour, not a dead-end. From the ashes of our heartbreak emerged resilience—a phoenix rising triumphant. We came to realize that every setback was, in truth, a setup for a comeback, and every closed door merely redirected us toward a new path. Thus armed with unwavering faith and fortified by love, we pressed forward on our journey, stepping boldly onto the uncharted path that lay before us, prepared to embrace whatever twists and turns life had in store.

Amidst the ceaseless demands, the perpetual tension of academia, and the high-pressure atmosphere of the healthcare sector, there existed an oasis in my life. This sanctuary of tranquility, of tacit comprehension, was none other than Pheona, my cherished companion, my confidante. Her spirit, steadfast like the undulating waves of the ocean, weathered the vicissitudes of life with a grace that rendered me speechless. As we traversed the perilous currents of the present, she stood as my guiding North Star, my beacon of hope amidst tempestuous seas.

Our bond transcended mere dreams and ambitions; it delved deep into the recesses of our pasts, embracing the pain that had shaped us into the individuals we had become. We found solace not only in the moments of exultant victory but also in the hushed spaces of mutual vulnerability.

Following our engagement in 2012, we embarked on the journey of planning our wedding. We chose to consecrate our love in the summer of 2013, amidst the benevolent gaze of God and the heartfelt blessings of our families. Our community, friends, and church congregation celebrated alongside us as we exchanged vows, pledging to navigate life's twists and turns together. Their jubilant amens and earnest prayers enveloped us like an early spring rain, a blissful benediction for our shared journey ahead.

Our journey, though intricate and multifaceted, bore witness to both moments of boundless joy and profound sorrow. Just a year into our marriage, we received the joyous news of impending parenthood. The prospect of welcoming our first child filled our hearts with unbridled anticipation. We envisioned the melodious laughter of our little one, the delightful disorder of toys strewn across our home, the tender scent of baby lotion, and the sheer magic of witnessing a new life unfold before our eyes. We eagerly awaited the arrival of our son, whom we affectionately named Desmond Junior, or DJ.

Our hopes of a future adorned with the soft shades of baby bliss were abruptly shattered by life's cruel hand. At eighteen weeks into the pregnancy, we were confronted with the devastating loss of DJ. In an instant, our world crumbled, shattered into a thousand fragments of shattered dreams. We found ourselves grappling with a pain so profound, so all-encompassing, it felt like being swallowed by an unfathomable abyss.

Our once vibrant apartment, resonant with plans of nursery décor and sweet lullabies, now stood cloaked in a deafening silence. It was a silence that screamed of an irreplaceable loss, a void that seemed to consume every corner of our existence. The absence of the child we had already begun to love left behind an agonizing hollowness, a void that echoed through the mundane rhythms of our daily lives.

In the midst of this tempest of sorrow, we discovered that we were not alone but encircled by an army of love. Our friends, family, and church community transformed into sturdy pillars of support, offering words of solace and gestures of affection that served as a soothing balm for our wounded hearts. Their tacit understanding and steadfast presence were like beams of light piercing through the darkness that enveloped us, offering us a glimmer of hope amidst the despair.

Our loss, while immensely painful, became a catalyst for strengthening the bond between us. We embraced our grief, recognizing it as a poignant testament to the love we held for DJ. Drawing closer together, we sought solace in shared memories and tears, finding comfort in each other's presence. With unwavering faith and love, we held onto hope, knowing that even in our darkest moments, our connection would serve as a guiding light through the shadows.

Our perspective shifted, allowing us to view each obstacle not as a barrier but as a chance for personal development. We recognized that adversity was not the end but a catalyst for growth, propelling us toward greater heights. Every setback became a setup for a comeback, guiding us along an alternate path filled with newfound opportunities. Our narrative was not reaching its conclusion; rather, it was embarking on a transformative journey toward a brighter future.

Our journey was evolving, transitioning into a new chapter filled with hope and resilience. While our story of loss was significant, it was just one part of a larger narrative awaiting exploration. Life, we discovered, was not solely about enduring hardships but also about embracing growth and flourishing despite adversity. With each step forward, hand in hand, we understood that every experience was molding us, equipping us for the adventures that lay ahead. This realization fueled our determination to embrace the journey with open hearts, knowing that this was not the conclusion, but merely the commencement of a new chapter.

NEW BEGINNINGS

Amidst the lingering grief of losing DJ, the news of Pheona's pregnancy brought a glimmer of hope, a flicker of light in the darkness. Though our hearts remained tender from the pain of our loss, they dared to beat with anticipation once again. This unexpected turn of events reinforced our understanding of life's complexity—a blend of sorrow and joy, of peaks and valleys, all intricately woven into the fabric of our existence.

In the early light of a radiant May morning in 2015, our first son entered the world. His initial cry, though soft and delicate, resonated with a vibrancy that pierced the quiet of the delivery room. To us, it was the most enchanting melody, a testament to the miracle of life. This symphony of existence echoed through the sterile hospital halls, touching the depths of our souls with its profound significance.

In that fleeting moment, our tears flowed freely, carrying with them a flood of emotions too immense to contain. They were tears of relief, of boundless joy, and of an unspoken love that enveloped us completely. In the quiet stillness of the room, as we held our son close, his tiny form became a symbol of our unwavering strength, his innocent gaze a promise of brighter days ahead.

Choosing the name Noah for our second son felt like a beacon of hope amidst the shadows of our past. It symbolized the promise of a new beginning, a fresh chapter in our lives filled with hope and optimism. My wife's wisdom and empathy guided us away from the path of sorrow, reminding us to cherish the memory of our firstborn while allowing our second son to forge his own identity. Noah's name became a testament to our resilience, a reminder that even in the darkest of times, there is always the promise of a brighter tomorrow.

Noah's presence brought a sense of renewal and vitality into our lives. Amidst the chaos of parenthood, his laughter and curiosity became our guiding light, leading us away from the darkness of grief and toward the promise of a brighter future. With each milestone he reached, from his first steps to his first words, our hearts swelled with pride and gratitude. Noah was not just our son; he was a symbol of hope, resilience, and the enduring power of love.

As the wheel of time turned, May 2016 marked a significant milestone for us. Noah was on the verge of celebrating his first birthday, and we were about to realize another dream of ours: purchasing our first home. The feeling was akin to conquering an emotional Everest. The triumph was punctuated by the sweet exhaustion that accompanies packing years of memories into boxes, transporting them across the city, and unloading them into a new space—a new beginning.

We moved into our new house just a few days before Noah's first birthday, marking the dawn of a fresh chapter in our life's story. The house, imbued with the scent of fresh paint and brimming with anticipation, whispered of boundless opportunities. Each room echoed with the potential for cherished memories yet to be woven, every wall a pristine canvas yearning to be adorned with the vibrant tapestry of our experiences. Our new home stood tall as a testament to our resilience, our unyielding faith, and the enduring love that formed the very foundation of our existence.

Our new home wasn't just a structure of bricks and mortar; it was a symbol of our hard work and relentless pursuit of the American Dream. Each brick in the wall, each plank of wood, each window, and door, bore testimony to the years of diligence, perseverance, and faith that had led us here. As we began to settle into our new house, we could see our dreams reflected in its corridors and our love embedded in its foundations.

The day we celebrated Noah's first birthday overflowed with profound gratitude. Watching our son bathed in the warm glow of candlelight, our hearts swelled with an inexplicable joy. This joy didn't merely stem from the milestones achieved or dreams realized; it emanated from the journey we'd undertaken, the battles fought, and the love that sustained us. Our story stands as a testament to love's power and resilience, a narrative woven with pain and triumph, loss and hope.

Every day with Noah proved a precious gift, a joyous exploration of life through his innocent eyes. His laughter served as the melody filling our home, his playful antics the tales that adorned our dinner table. Witnessing his growth, learning, and exploration, we too evolved alongside him, discovering the world anew through the prism of his unbridled joy and boundless curiosity.

As we progressed in our journey, our hearts bore the memories of our past, not as painful scars but as badges of honor. The pain we endured had morphed into resilience, the loss we experienced into enduring love. Aware that the road ahead held its share of peaks and valleys, joys and sorrows, we found solace in each other's presence. With one another, we believed we could weather any storm, conquer any mountain, traverse any valley.

Our lives, once a canvas of black and white, had transformed into a vibrant mosaic of colors, each hue embodying a moment, a memory, a milestone. Each passing day introduced fresh challenges, lessons, joys, and dreams. Reflecting on our journey, we recognized that our story was far from complete. Our past served as a prologue to our present, and our present, we believed, was laying the groundwork for a future brimming with promise and potential.

Our lives, once disrupted by a storm of grief, now hummed with a melody of hope, resonating with the rhythms of love, resilience, and faith. Through the fires of loss, we walked, emerging not unscathed, but fortified—stronger, wiser, more compassionate. The tapestry of our lives, once frayed and faded, now wove with threads of gold, each strand a moment of triumph, a milestone achieved, a dream realized.

As we journeyed forward, hand in hand, heart to heart, we recognized that the chapters of our story were penned by the greatest author of all—Life itself. With each turn of the page, with every sunrise and sunset, we discovered that our narrative, woven with its unique blend of sorrow and joy, pain and triumph, stood as a testament to the remarkable power of love, faith, and resilience. It remained, and continues to be, our very own American Dream.

The raw authenticity of our journey stamped itself onto the landscape of our lives. Our American Dream wasn't crafted from effortless triumphs or smooth voyages. Instead, it emerged as a mosaic of setbacks, challenges, hope, resilience, and unwavering faith. Within each hurdle, we unearthed opportunities to evolve, to glean wisdom, and to emerge fortified.

Noah's early years brimmed with innocent joy, marked by first words, first steps, and endless laughter. His curious eyes shimmered with life, reflecting our wonder and gratitude. As Noah blossomed, so did we, transforming from two individuals bound by love into parents whose universe centered around a tiny, demanding, yet utterly delightful human being. The weariness from sleepless nights, the persistent concern over missed meals or delayed milestones, the elation of his inaugural word—these were the threads weaving the fabric of our existence.

Throughout our journey together, we've gleaned the significance of gratitude, the strength of faith, and the vitality of resilience. We've navigated life's ebbs and flows, weathered its trials and celebrated its triumphs, all of which have molded our course. Yet, amid it all, we've clung steadfastly to our belief in the American Dream—not merely a quest for success or material riches, but a pursuit of a life abundant in love, resilience, and purpose.

Our story, our journey, serves as a testament to the truth that the American Dream isn't a one-size-fits-all mold. It's as varied as the individuals who dare to dream it. For us, it meant constructing a life from the ground up, drawing strength from our past, navigating our present realities, and envisioning our future aspirations. It entailed bridging the chasm between our current state and our desired destination.

In the grand tapestry of the American Dream, we are but a small fragment. Yet, in our own humble way, we've left an indelible mark on the canvas of our lives. Our journey persists, and with each passing day, we draw nearer to the realization of our dreams. We carry with us the memories of our past, the realities of our present, and the aspirations for our future. Our existence stands as living proof that the American Dream, though challenging at times, is within reach with resilience, diligence, and unwavering faith.

6

The Seed of Change

Alan Watts' impactful words, "The only way to make sense out of change is to plunge into it, move with it, and join the dance," resonate deeply with me. They serve as a guiding light throughout my journey, particularly in Chapter 6, "The Seed of Change." Within these pages, I explore the transformative moments that have shaped my trajectory—a journey marked by adversity, loss, and an unwavering commitment to effecting meaningful change in the world.

The loss of my grandmother served as a crucible moment, fundamentally altering my perception of the world. Emerging from the crucible of war's hardships and personal loss, I embraced a newfound aspiration: to reach out, to connect, and to aid others. Within this chapter lies a chronicle of transformation, spotlighting the pivotal experiences that reshaped my outlook and forged my purpose.

Through a narrative of self-discovery, I extend an invitation for you to journey alongside me as I navigate the twin forces of pain and joy, utilizing them as catalysts for transformation. From moments of deep introspection to the dawning realization of purpose, "The Seed of Change" chronicles my evolution from a youth molded by adversity to an adult committed to instigating change within myself and the broader world.

As we journey through this chapter together, you'll witness how the seeds of change, initially sown in the fertile soil of adversity, can blossom and bring about profound transformations in our lives. This tale isn't solely mine; it serves as a testament to the growth, resilience, and boundless potential for transformation inherent in each of us.

Join me on this journey of sowing the seeds of change—seeds that, nurtured with hope, resilience, and care, will grow rapidly into a flourishing tree of personal and collective growth. Welcome to "The Seed of Change."

GROWTH AND TRANSFORMATION

Transitioning from the war-torn streets of Liberia to the unfamiliar corridors of an American high school marked the beginning of a different kind of battle for me—not one defined by violence, but by mockery. As a young immigrant, this shift was profound. The halls I navigated became a stage for ridicule, contrasting sharply with the struggles I had endured back home. However, instead of breaking me, the taunts in an American high school served as a catalyst for transformation.

This experience laid the groundwork for profound empathy towards those silently struggling, fueling a passion to pursue a career dedicated to offering support and understanding to those adrift in challenging environments, much like myself. Navigating through the complexities of higher education, questioning my place within it, and grappling with rejection from a social work program, I encountered a setback that would eventually guide me toward my true calling in psychology.

The path I've traveled, adorned with both the scars of ridicule and the triumphs of overcoming, illustrates the poignant paradox of my journey—a fusion of introspection and outward exploration. As day turned to night and the vibrant hues of sunsets surrendered to the velvet embrace of night skies, my self-awareness blossomed. In those tranquil moments, attuned to the wind's gentle whispers and the rhythmic cadence of my heartbeat, I unearthed my purpose: to aid others in navigating the labyrinth of their minds.

The encouragement from my wife acted as the catalyst for this revelation, stirring the still waters of my thoughts and igniting a desire to channel the turmoil of my past into a force for aiding others. This prospect, simultaneously exciting and daunting, felt akin to a guiding hand steering me toward a glimmer of light amidst the darkness.

My journey to this current role was filled with challenges. College became a battleground where I grappled with doubts about my belonging and fit within the mental health profession. These feelings of uncertainty were not unfamiliar; they echoed the sentiments I faced when applying for the social work program at Northeastern State University (NSU). Despite submitting a carefully crafted application that drew from my experiences as a troubled youth in Liberia, the rejection I encountered was a bitter pill to swallow. Being denied admission based on supposedly unmet requirements forced me to question the value of my experiences and my identity as a minority striving for impact. However, it was precisely this setback that steered me toward psychology and mental health, a field that would soon reveal itself as my true calling.

Life, however, had another obstacle in store. The rejection from the social work program was a harsh blow, yet it underscored the notion that success resembles a mosaic—each piece, whether a failure or victory, contributes to the greater picture. This pivotal moment in my journey compelled me to reassess my goals, strengths, and determination, teaching me that detours often lead us to our destined paths.

Immersing myself deeply into the realm of psychology, I embarked on an exploration of territories previously unknown to me. Each topic I studied seemed like a reflection of my own story, allowing me to revisit my life's journey through the perspective of psychological principles. This exploration brought me comfort and a sense of connection, revealing the intricate ways in which our individual experiences are intertwined with universal human conditions. Psychology became a gateway to understanding the collective nature of our experiences, emphasizing the commonalities that bind us despite our unique stories.

The decision to pursue a degree in psychology felt like aligning with the cosmos. Each class, every professor, and every peer became integral to my transformation. My initial encounter with social psychology acted as a mirror, reflecting on the person I had become through the trials I had faced and overcome.

The turning point in my journey arrived on December 6, 2016, a day draped in a surreal atmosphere. The auditorium pulsed with anticipation and excitement, reflecting the turbulent yet jubilant whirlwind within me. When my name echoed through the hall, followed by applause, it felt like a symphony encapsulating my journey of resilience and optimism. With my degree in hand, I stood as proof of the power of persistence, a guiding light for those who dare to dream in the face of adversity.

The sight of my family, glowing with pride and joy, flooded me with overwhelming gratitude. Their steadfast belief in me, their unwavering support through every trial, and their sacrifices marked the apex of this important chapter in my life. They served as my unwavering beacon through every storm, the calm amidst turmoil, and the wellspring of my fortitude when uncertainty threatened to overwhelm me.

From the resilience cultivated in the streets of West Point to standing at the point of realizing the American Dream, my journey stands as a testament to the potency of enduring hope and unwavering determination. As I assumed my mantle as a mental health provider, I carried with me not just the teachings of my past, but also the aspirations for a future brimming with potential. I emerged as a fusion of resilience, faith, hope, love, and indomitable spirit, poised to effectuate a profound impact on the world.

This transition into the field of psychology heralded the commencement of a fresh chapter imbued with purpose and fervor. Recalling my graduation, I was inundated with the intense emotions of that day—the elation, the expectancy, and the profound sense of accomplishment. Poised at the precipice of a new journey, I was equipped with my past encounters, fueled by resilience, and spurred onward by the dreams that had guided me thus far.

A profound sense of fulfillment enveloped this new journey. The commitment and diligence that had molded my academic trajectory were on the verge of fruition, heralding a future wherein I could profoundly influence lives. What was once a tale marred by adversity had evolved into a narrative of hope and empowerment, standing as a guiding light for others traversing their own paths amidst life's trials.

The journey toward a career in clinical mental health counseling proved to be as challenging as it was rewarding. The University of Oklahoma served as a vibrant tapestry of academia, a melting pot of diverse cultures, a hub of intellectual vigor, and a bastion of inclusivity where personal growth seamlessly intertwined with professional advancement. With anticipation and curiosity coursing through my veins, I embarked on this new expedition.

Reflecting on my journey, from the chaotic streets of Liberia to the tranquil suburbs of Oklahoma, I am overwhelmed with a sense of achievement and thankfulness. I am more than just a survivor of hardships; I am a testament to resilience, faith, and an unshakeable belief in my aspirations. As I progress in my career, my commitment to aiding others in navigating their mental health obstacles remains unwavering. I eagerly anticipate a future where mental health is destigmatized and recognized as integral to our overall well-being—a world where compassion prevails over prejudice and understanding eclipses ignorance. My journey presses on, and I am prepared to embrace whatever lies ahead.

Looking back, my journey—complete with setbacks, anguish, trials, resilience, and triumph—has sculpted me into the individual I am today. I am no longer the boy who narrowly evaded the grip of civil wars. I am no longer the teenager who caused his parents countless sleepless nights. I am no longer merely the young man who pursued the elusive American Dream.

I had emerged as a beacon of hope, an embodiment of resilience, a testament to the notion that our past does not dictate our future, but rather shapes us into the individuals we are destined to become. I had embraced the belief that every adversity presents an opportunity for personal growth, and every setback serves as a stepping stone toward triumph.

As I press onward in my journey, I hold close the lessons I've absorbed, the encounters I've encountered, and the love and faith that have steered me forward. My aim is to share these with the world around me, to assist others in navigating their own paths, and to illuminate the way for those ensnared in darkness. I am now the counselor who lends a hand, the father who offers unconditional love, the husband who provides unwavering support, and the individual who persists in learning, evolving, inspiring, and motivating others.

JOURNEY TO MENTAL HEALTH: BECOMING A THERAPIST

My Journey into the realm of mental health sprung from a profound desire to help others—a fervor rooted in my journey of adversity and perseverance. In my role as a case manager, I encountered individuals from diverse backgrounds, united by the thread of mental illness. These interactions, brimming with shared vulnerabilities, resonated with my past tribulations, igniting a fervent resolve to uplift those trapped in the shadows of societal stigma and personal misery. This position transcended mere support; it was a journey of perpetual education and development, wherein my experiences illuminated a path of hope for those I endeavored to assist.

Several events served as catalysts for my choice to pursue a career in mental health, but none were more influential than the reports of numerous school shootings across the United States. These tragedies, coupled with my encounters during the war and witnessing the struggles of young men and child soldiers profoundly affected by the aftermath of the Liberian civil conflict, left an unforgettable mark on me. The atrocities and cries of innocent lives lost shook me to my very foundation. They underscored the pivotal role mental health plays in our society and intensified my determination to effect change in this domain.

Another significant influence was a vivid childhood memory etched into the depths of my mind. While growing up in Liberia, I vividly recall observing a man in our community who appeared to be suffering from schizophrenia. The stigma enveloping him, the mocking glimpses, the whispered labels of 'madman' and 'crazy', the social isolation—these images left an lasting imprint on my consciousness, igniting my fervor to combat such stereotypes and instigate transformation.

The adage 'you can't run from your calling' resonated deeply with me during my application process for a position at CREOKS, an organization offering services to both children and adults. Initially, I aimed for a role on the children's side, motivated by a recommendation from a close friend and former classmate from graduate school. With the details somewhat unclear, I eagerly submitted my application, unaware of the precise nature of the position I had chosen.

Upon arriving for the interview, a blend of nervousness and uncertainty wrapped me, heightened by the unexpected sight of a room bustling with employees. Initially, a wave of apprehension swept over me, fearing I had veered off course. However, the warm reception from the staff, especially the individual who had liaised with me over the phone, gradually assuaged my unease. Their amiable demeanor during this preliminary interaction served to alleviate the tension in the air.

As the interview officially commenced, Rachel initiated a round of introductions, inviting each person in the room to share a bit about themselves. This approach fostered a personal and interactive atmosphere, setting a welcoming tone for the discussion. Following this, a series of questions were posed by at least five individuals, delving into my motivations and suitability for the role.

After a successful interview, during which I navigated the questions with confidence, I was promptly offered the position. Despite my initial application being geared towards a role involving children, fate had a different trajectory in store for me. I was presented with an opportunity on the adult side of CREOKS Behavioral Health Services, owing to a new Certified Community Behavioral Health Clinic (CCBHC) grant that required additional staffing. It was at this crucial juncture that I decided to embrace the role of an adult case manager—a path that deviated from my original intent but resonated with equal conviction.

Accepting the case manager position marked the onset of my journey in mental health—a domain that not only deeply influenced my own life but also brought immense joy and fulfillment. This transition wasn't just a career change; it symbolized a significant leap into a profession that resonated with me on a personal level, fueled by a genuine connection and an unwavering passion to effect positive change in the lives of those we support.

The choice to transition working with adults was shaped not only by the organizational requirements but also by my professional evolution. Although Rachel played a pivotal role in my interview process, it was Ashley, to whom I would directly report. Despite not having prior experience working with Ashley, her reputation as a supportive and adept leader decided to join her team as a straightforward one.

Ashley, who later joined my interview, extended the offer for me to be a part of her team in adult services. This unforeseen twist paved the way for a significant and fulfilling chapter in my career at CREOKS. Under Ashley's guidance, I wholeheartedly embraced the challenges and opportunities inherent in the adult case manager role, actively contributing to the organization's mission while also reaping the rewards of a supportive and enriching work environment.

In my capacity as a case manager, I engaged with individuals from diverse backgrounds who were confronting mental health obstacles. Every interaction, every narrative shared, and every moment spent with them imparted invaluable lessons. I swiftly recognized that my role extended beyond offering assistance; rather, they served as catalysts for my growth as both a professional and a person, endowing me with a profound comprehension of the human experience.

I immersed myself in the intricate and occasionally unsettling realm of mental health. It proved to be a demanding role, necessitating unwavering patience, boundless empathy, and an indomitable determination to effect change. As I traversed through this uncharted chapter of my life, the sense of purpose that had previously eluded me now embraced me fully. Each day served as a testament to my resilience, my faith, and the enduring strength of the human spirit.

As my journey with CREOKS continued, a fresh opportunity arose that reignited my initial passion—working with children. This shift materialized through an opening for a school-based therapist role, a position I enthusiastically embraced. Now, nearly two years into working with children, I look back on my experiences with profound gratitude. The leadership and camaraderie at CREOKS, spanning both children's and adult services, have been remarkably supportive, cultivating a work environment that is both nurturing and empowering.

Today, there's a playful jest among us about how Ashley 'stole' me from the children's side, only for Rachel to 'take me back,' highlighting the light-hearted dynamics and strong bonds within our team. It's as if I couldn't escape my calling, a sentiment that underscores the destined nature of my journey and the fulfillment I find in my work. Every aspect of my time at CREOKS, from the unexpected shifts in roles to the current satisfaction I derive from my position, serves as a testament to the organization's dynamic and responsive nature. Contributing to such a welcoming and forward-thinking community has been a privilege, and I eagerly anticipate continuing my journey with them.

In the summer of 2022, as I received my master's degree in clinical mental health counseling, the moment felt utterly surreal. Amidst the vast expanse of the auditorium, the resounding applause swelled, engulfing me as I made my way to the stage. The atmosphere was electric with celebration, my name echoing amidst a sea of faces—friends, family, and members of my church who had congregated to commemorate this milestone. Their unwavering support enveloped me like a tangible wave of euphoria, underscoring the profound significance of the moment. At this pivotal juncture, my life was enriched not only by academic accomplishment but also by the joyful responsibility of parenthood. My wife and I were blessed with four incredible children: Noah, Nathan, Naomi, and Nehemiah. Each of them, a divine blessing, stood as a beacon of pride, their faces illuminated with joy as they witnessed their father's commendation. This ceremony transcended mere personal achievement; it was a collective celebration of progress, a testament to the journey undertaken and the dreams yet to be realized.

With the completion of my master's degree, my journey with CREOKS Behavioral Health Services evolved from being a case manager to taking on the responsibilities of a mental health counselor and therapist. This transition was guided by the trust and rapport I had built over the years, illuminating my path toward further professional development.

After successfully passing my national counselor exam and receiving approval from the Oklahoma Board of Behavioral Health, I commenced my supervision. The end of my supervision signified the final strides toward obtaining licensure as a professional counselor in Oklahoma—a journey that unexpectedly brought me back into the realm of education. However, this time, I wasn't a student but rather a pillar of support. Serving as an embedded mental health counselor in a high school, I found myself in a unique position to extend empathy and guidance to students grappling with their challenges. My past encounters with ridicule had evolved into a valuable tool, empowering me to authentically connect with and support these young individuals.

The pursuit of my licensure as a professional counselor marked a phase of profound self-discovery and growth. Guided by my Board Approved Supervisor, Brian—an esteemed professional both respected and formidable—I embarked on a journey of introspection. This stage wasn't merely about honing my skills; it was also about confronting and transcending my insecurities and biases and understanding the importance of embracing constructive criticism with humility and grace.

The unexpected shift in my career path, transitioning to work within a high school, initially seemed incongruent with my original aspiration of focusing on outpatient therapy for adults. However, upon deeper reflection, I discerned a profound connection between my adolescent struggles in Liberia and the challenges faced by the students I now endeavored to support. My journey, characterized by its own trials and tribulations, was not solely about personal growth, but also about equipping me to make a meaningful impact on the lives of young individuals grappling with similar issues within a vastly different context.

Embracing my role within the high school felt like embracing my destiny. The transition from a troubled teenager in Liberia to becoming a mental health counselor for American youth underscored the intricate ways in which our past experiences shape our future contributions. My work in the school, emphasizing the critical need for mental health support, became a source of profound personal fulfillment. It served as a constant reminder of the importance of giving back—a principle deeply ingrained in my journey from adversity to advocacy. Each day reaffirms the idea that our struggles can be transformed into opportunities to aid others, highlighting the invaluable lessons we've gleaned from our past in shaping a more promising future for those we are privileged to serve.

As a therapist, my journey has uniquely equipped me to engage with a diverse array of individuals navigating mental and behavioral health hurdles. This role has humbled and enriched me profoundly, evolving me from a boy in Liberia, intimately acquainted with adversity, into a professional empowered to effect meaningful change. The opportunity to serve and contribute has imbued me with a profound sense of purpose, reinforcing the importance of giving back.

Today, as I traverse the hallways of a high school, I stand not as an outsider but as a pivotal ally for those in need. My transformation from a troubled youth and a subject of ridicule to a resilient advocate for mental health underscores the transformative influence of our past experiences on our present and future. It serves as a vivid illustration of how resilience can transmute adversity into a potent tool for assisting others.

Reflecting on my life's journey, I've come to realize that every challenge, every triumph, has been guiding me toward a greater purpose. My story stands as a testament to the potential for transformation and the profound impact an individual can have in their community and beyond.

Looking ahead, the path I walk is brimming with promise.

My commitment to aiding others on their mental health journey remains a driving force of inspiration. I envision expanding my endeavors beyond Oklahoma to Liberia, my birthplace, aspiring to bolster mental health awareness and support there. My life embodies a cycle of receiving, growing, and compassionately giving back.

Bringing my narrative to the present moment, I frequently ponder the trajectory that has brought me to this juncture. The chapters of my life, once overshadowed by fear and turmoil, have converged into a story of tranquility, purpose, and steadfastness. Despite the trials endured, I harbor no resentment, acknowledging that these experiences have strengthened my determination, cultivated my empathy, and guided me to where I stand today.

The journey has been rife with challenges, each obstacle serving as a lesson in resilience and perseverance. The unwavering support of my wife Pheona, my children, my parents, and my community has been the bedrock of my capacity to navigate these trials.

As I press onward, the lessons gleaned from my past serve as a sturdy foundation for my dedication to mental health advocacy. My journey, from the slums of West Point to my current role as a mental health professional, epitomizes the potency of hope and resilience. Each day, as I discharge my responsibilities as a counselor, I am propelled by a steadfast belief in my capacity to enact positive change.

My future is unequivocal: to serve, to learn, and to evolve. I am committed to advancing mental health awareness, particularly in communities where it remains a stigmatized subject. My aspirations are focused on effecting change in Liberia, facilitating understanding and management of mental health issues.

I share my story as a beacon of hope for anyone embarking on their life journey. It's a message that, irrespective of one's starting point or the challenges encountered, each of us possesses the ability to shape our destiny. I stand as a living testament that one's origins do not dictate their future. Remember, every setback is simply a prelude to a magnificent comeback.

As I press forward, I carry with me a quote by Charles Darwin that deeply resonates with my experiences: "It is not the strongest of the species that survives, nor the most intelligent. It is the one most adaptable to change." This sentiment encapsulates my life's journey, serving as a constant reminder of my growth, resilience, and unwavering determination to evolve from a boy of the slums into a man of purpose. My narrative is far from complete; indeed, I am eager to embrace what the future holds. Though I have come a considerable distance, my journey persists, brimming with anticipation for the chapters yet to unfold.

Reflecting on my journey, I am overwhelmed with a profound sense of gratitude. Gratitude for the trials and tribulations that sculpted me, for the individuals who placed their faith in me, and for the dreams that illuminated my path. I haven't merely survived; I've flourished, discovering my purpose amidst chaos and forging a path that is distinctly my own. I've transcended my past, embraced my present, and eagerly anticipate a future brimming with endless possibilities.

My life, akin to a captivating tapestry, has been woven with countless hues - some vibrant, some muted, some shadowed. Yet, every thread and every color contributes to the overall design, rendering it complete, making it uniquely mine. From the war-scarred streets of Liberia to the flourishing heartland of America, my journey embodies resilience, fortitude, and the indomitable human spirit. As I stand here today, gazing toward the horizon, I recognize that my story is far from its conclusion. It is merely the beginning. With anticipation, I turn the page to the next chapter, firmly believing that the best is yet to come.

7

Rising from the Ashes

"THE GREATEST GLORY IN LIVING LIES NOT IN NEVER
FALLING, BUT IN RISING EVERY TIME WE FALL."
– NELSON MANDELA

The dawn of a new chapter often brings forth a profound sense of anticipation, symbolizing the end of one era and the commencement of another. This sentiment precisely captured my emotions as I received my master's degree in clinical mental health counseling from the University of Oklahoma. Amidst the jubilant atmosphere and the resounding cheers of fellow graduates, I stood—a testament to relentless determination and hope, a young man who had traversed from the tumultuous streets of West Point to this pinnacle of triumph.

This chapter of my life transcends mere recollection of professional and academic accomplishments; it embodies a tale of profound personal metamorphosis. Memories of my past, brimming with trials and triumphs, emphasize the resilience that propelled me onward. This resilience transcended mere survival; it ignited a profound calling to nurture, empathize, and support those entangled in their mental health struggles.

Joining CREOKS Behavioral Health Services as a case manager afforded me the opportunity to witness the breadth of human resilience. From veterans grappling with PTSD to single mothers combatting depression, each interaction underscored the universal battle with mental health challenges and emphasized the critical importance of empathy and support.

Transitioning to a therapist role, especially within a high school environment, marked a full-circle moment for me. Interacting with students, I recognized echoes of my own journey in their struggles, further solidifying my dedication to offering support and compassion. This phase of my career went beyond mere counseling; it evolved into a testament to the transformative influence of empathy.

Earning my license from the Oklahoma State Behavioral Health Board signified the fulfillment of a long-held aspiration. This accomplishment represented more than just a professional milestone; it epitomized the culmination of a journey devoted to effecting a meaningful impact on mental health care.

Reflecting on this journey fills me with humility and gratitude. From enduring adversity in Liberia to becoming a beacon of hope for those grappling with mental health challenges, my story epitomizes the cyclical nature of growth and giving back. This narrative celebrates overcoming obstacles, transforming past trials into stepping stones for future successes, and reaffirms the pivotal role of resilience in shaping one's destiny.

From the tumult of Liberia to the academic corridors of Oklahoma, and onward into the realm of mental health counseling, my journey exemplifies the human spirit's remarkable capacity for transformation. Now, on the cusp of a new chapter as a licensed mental health provider, I am eager to persist in my mission of service, learning, and advocacy, aspiring to explore horizons yet undiscovered.

This narrative, my phoenix story, narrates the rebirth from the ashes of adversity, aiming to inspire others to envision beyond their present circumstances and unlock their potential for transformation. My past, punctuated by brushes with mental illness and personal tribulations, has profoundly shaped my professional ethos—driving me to aid others in their mental health odysseys, guided by a tale of resilience and rejuvenation.

Now, as a newly graduated individual with my diploma grasped firmly in hand, enveloped by the steadfast support of friends, family, and my church community, I feel a profound tether to my past and a radiant vision for my future. My tenure at CREOKS, starting as a case manager and now blossoming into a therapist, mirrors a voyage defined by education, evolution, and an unshakeable dedication to those requiring assistance.

This transformative journey was illuminated by every person I've crossed paths with, each narrative of hardship and resilience, and every instance of connection and empathy. My story, from navigating the challenges of Liberia to championing mental health advocacy, encapsulates the faith in transformation and the influence of a single individual. I persist in emerging from the ashes of my past, resolute to illuminate the path for others on their mental health expedition, embodying the metamorphosis that characterizes my phoenix narrative—a tale of renewal, hope, and lasting influence.

In this chapter titled "Rising from the Ashes," I invite you to embark on a journey of profound transformation with me. Much like a phoenix, I have emerged from the debris of my past, reborn and redefined by the fires of adversity. This chapter unveils the path I traversed, evolving from a struggling immigrant student in a foreign land, through the unwavering quest for enlightenment, culminating in a flourishing scholar fervently devoted to a life of service. Let us embark on this journey together.

My aspiration to aid others wrestling with mental health difficulties took root with the distressing news of a school shooting incident in the United States. It ignited a fervent impulse within me, a profound need to contribute, to effect change, and to utilize my journey as a guide to assist others in shaping their narratives of triumph over adversity. This intense desire propelled me down an unforeseen path, to the University of Oklahoma, Tulsa, where I elected to pursue a graduate degree in clinical mental health counseling.

Experiences from my past in Liberia played a pivotal role in shaping this decision. I vividly remember the homeless man, affectionately referred to as "Mon ami" or "my friend" in French, who resided on Newport Street, a mere stone's throw away from Mamba Point. He was a constant presence, his ongoing self-conversations and erratic behavior, now recognized as symptoms of schizophrenia, lending an aura of intrigue to our childhood pastimes. We would observe him from a cautious distance, uncertain of his unpredictable actions, yet captivated by his uniqueness.

Fast forward a decade, and there I stood, proudly clutching my master's degree in clinical mental health counseling from the esteemed University of Oklahoma. Reflecting on my journey, it felt surreal, marked by numerous obstacles and invaluable, life-altering teachings. Surrounding me were my cherished loved ones - friends, family, and members of my church - who gathered to celebrate my triumph. Their exuberant cheers echoed in my ears as I proudly hoisted my degree aloft.

During this momentous period, my wife and I were bestowed with the extraordinary gift of four beautiful children. Noah, Nathan, Naomi, and Nehemiah, each a manifestation of love and a symbol of hope, brought immeasurable joy into our lives. As I reflected on this remarkable full-circle journey, I marveled at the profound transformation. A boy from Liberia, who had weathered trials and adversity, now stood before the world as a graduate, a counselor, and a father, prepared to leverage his experiences to aid others.

Following my graduation from Northeastern State University with a Bachelor of Science degree in psychology, I embarked on my journey as a case manager at CREOKS. This marked my initial foray into the realm of mental health—a stark departure from my upbringing in Liberia, where such roles were unfamiliar, and the notion of mental health was often shrouded in stigma.

In Liberia, the perception of mental health was often clouded by ignorance and fear. Individuals grappling with mental health issues were frequently dismissed as weak or, in more extreme cases, believed to be possessed by evil spirits. Only recently, with the rise of global awareness initiatives, has Africa begun to confront and comprehend mental health challenges. Despite the cultural shift necessary, I felt compelled to embrace this leap into the field of mental health.

As a case manager, I engaged with individuals from diverse backgrounds, each grappling with their mental health struggles. I discovered that socioeconomic status held little significance in the realm of mental health. Embracing my role, I utilized it as a platform to empower these individuals and provide a guiding light of hope.

Following the attainment of my master's degree, I embarked on the next phase of my journey at CREOKS, assuming the role of a mental health counselor and therapist. Assigned as a school-based therapist, I found this experience to be profoundly enriching. It afforded me the opportunity to deliver mental health counseling services to high school students, a responsibility that I held dear to my heart.

Every interaction, every moment of progress, and every triumph achieved by these young individuals filled me with an indescribable sense of fulfillment. The gratification I experienced from aiding these young minds in navigating their mental health journeys was boundless. It served as a driving force, motivating me to pursue my national board certification exam and complete my 3,000 supervision hours. This milestone propelled me forward on the journey toward becoming a licensed mental health provider in the state of Oklahoma.

Now, as a licensed professional counselor, I feel privileged to offer support to individuals grappling with a diverse array of mental health conditions. My journey from Liberia to this point serves as a testament to the profound impact one can have in this field. Additionally, my wife and I have been blessed with five precious children—three boys and two girls—who bring immeasurable joy and fulfillment to our lives.

I am firmly convinced that I was destined for this path, serving as living proof of the remarkable capacity for change and the profound impact one person can have in the world. With each individual I assist and every life I touch, I am fulfilling my life's mission. The metaphor of the phoenix is fitting—I have indeed risen from the ashes of my past, soaring towards a future brimming with hope, healing, and an unwavering commitment to make a positive difference in the lives of others.

8

Lighting the Path

"DO NOT WAIT FOR LEADERS; DO IT ALONE, PERSON TO PERSON." – MOTHER TERESA

Every journey inevitably encounters a crucial moment—a crossroad where the traveler, once entangled in the thickets of the unknown, pauses, pivots, and emerges as a beacon, illuminating the path for others. In the eighth chapter of this memoir, titled "Lighting the Path," this juncture comes to fruition. Here, it transcends mere storytelling; it morphs into a guiding light, navigating others through their odyssey of resilience, transformation, and self-realization. In this chapter, my narrative shifts from a tale of personal conquest to assuming the role of a catalyst for change, steering fellow voyagers through their turbulent waters.

Join me as we embark on a voyage together, tracing the trajectory from my humble beginnings as a resilient yet confused immigrant to my emergence as an advocate for resilience and emotional well-being. Within the pages of "Lighting the Path," you'll witness not just my evolution, but also the reflections of the lives I've encountered and the souls I aspire to ignite with hope and courage.

As we delve into this chapter, we journey through my postgraduate years, a period where I transformed my resilience into a structured model. This model, a mosaic woven from my experiences, struggles, and triumphs, serves as a testament to how my journey evolved into a mission to empower others to face their adversities.

In "Lighting the Path," we unveil the genesis of the **RESILIENCE model**—a brainchild conceived from the tapestry of my odyssey, fueled by academic dedication, and ignited by an unwavering desire to catalyze positive change. Within these pages, you'll bear witness to the trials and triumphs of crafting this model, the victories seized, and the invaluable lessons garnered along the way.

Join me in "Lighting the Path" as we traverse from the bustling streets of Liberia to the serene classrooms of Oklahoma, showcasing the practical application of Ginsburg's 7C's of resilience and Seligman's groundbreaking work on learned optimism. Within this chapter, we seamlessly intertwine evidence-based practices from cognitive-behavioral therapy, illustrating how the transformation of maladaptive thought patterns can cultivate resilience in the face of adversity.

In essence, my resilience model reflects my journey and offers a roadmap for nurturing resilience. It encapsulates the lessons learned from my own experiences, fortified by psychological research and unwavering determination. As you journey through my memoir, I aspire for you to discover within my resilience model a guiding light for your path—an arsenal of tools to navigate adversity and cultivate resilience.

At the core of "Lighting the Path" lies a testament to the profound impact of generosity, the catalyst for change, and the profound fulfillment found in guiding others. It serves as a vivid portrayal of the transformative force of resilience—the remarkable potential concealed within adversity, poised to be harnessed for change. Let us always remember: every story we write, every path we illuminate, possesses the extraordinary power to guide, inspire, and ignite transformation.

Resilience, the capacity to rebound from adversity and flourish, has long been a focal point of research and inquiry among scholars (APA, 2019). Within this domain, two figures stand prominently: Dr. Kenneth Ginsburg and Dr. Martin Seligman. Their seminal works have played pivotal roles in advancing our comprehension of resilience and its mechanisms.

In developing this *Resilience Model*, I've drawn heavily from the inspiring works of renowned psychologists like Dr. Kenneth Ginsburg and Dr. Martin Seligman, coupled with my personal experiences and insights. This synergy between empirical research and lived experience has led to a model that is as empirically sound as it is personally significant.

Dr. Ginsburg's 7C's of resilience—competence, confidence, connection, character, contribution, coping, and control—resonate deeply with the narratives woven throughout my memoir. In my model, competence and confidence manifest through the depiction of my personal and academic growth amidst adversity. The emphasis on connection is evident in the bonds forged and nurtured—from the bustling streets of Liberia to the diverse communities I encountered in Oklahoma.

Dr. Seligman's pioneering research on learned optimism and resilience serves as a cornerstone of my model, notably resonating with its "hope" and "dreams" pillars. His concepts advocate for cultivating a positive outlook and nurturing aspirations, which are fundamental in fostering resilience.

In essence, my resilience model serves as both a reflection of my past and a blueprint for cultivating resilience. It encapsulates the lessons gleaned from my personal journey, grounded in rigorous psychological research and unwavering determination. As you journey through my memoir, I hope you discover within my resilience model a roadmap for your own transformative journey. May it equip you with the tools needed to navigate adversity and nurture your resilience."

At the heart of this chapter lies a testament to the profound impact of generosity, the exhilaration of inspiring change, and the deep fulfillment derived from guiding others. It embodies the transformative potency of resilience, showcasing the remarkable potential latent within adversity, waiting to be harnessed and wielded as a catalyst for change. As we embark on this journey through the chapter, let us remember: every path we illuminate, every story we tell, possesses the remarkable power to guide, inspire, and ignite change.

Life, in its myriad forms, resembles an expedition through uncharted terrain—a voyage marked by unforeseen twists, peaks and valleys, moments of elation and despair. Each journey is unique, every path distinct, yet woven into the fabric of our existence is a common thread—the intrinsic human ability to adapt, to persevere, and to flourish in the face of adversity. This universal capacity for resilience forms the bedrock of this chapter, the cornerstone upon which 'Lighting the Path' is constructed.

The *RESILIENCE model* is built on principles shaped from the bedrock of my experiences and buttressed by scientific research. It is a living testament to my journey and serves as a compass, guiding others toward resilience and emotional well-being. Each letter stands for a principle that has been pivotal in my journey, together forming the roadmap for resilience:

Recognize the Journey (R): This pillar underscores the importance of acknowledging the trials and triumphs that have shaped our present reality. Growing up in Liberia evokes memories of navigating bustling markets under the scorching sun of West Point. Our home, though makeshift, served as a sanctuary amidst the chaos, shielding my family from the harsh elements and echoes of gunfire. Despite the civil unrest that gripped our streets, we remained resilient, refusing to succumb to despair.

Embrace the Shift (E): This pillar emphasizes the importance of embracing change and adaptation, drawing strength from past experiences to navigate new challenges. Life in Monrovia provided early lessons in resilience, preparing me for the seismic shifts yet to come. From mastering survival skills amidst the civil wars in Liberia to acclimating to the cultural shift of relocating to the United States, I learned to embrace change with open arms.

Strategize for Triumph (S): This pillar underscores the importance of strategic thinking and perseverance in overcoming adversity. In Liberia, my family and I relied on strategic planning to navigate the challenges of wartime scarcity, ensuring our survival amidst adversity. Transitioning to life in America presented a new battleground, where academic excellence became the focal point of our strategic efforts.

Ignite Transformation (I): Transformation indeed lies at the heart of resilience—a lesson I learned most profoundly at the outset of my journey in the mental health field. With each client I encountered and every story I heard; a profound metamorphosis ignited within me. I came to grasp the vast expanse and profound depth of human resilience, recognizing how each struggle possesses the potential to kindle personal growth. Gradually, I began to perceive the flames of adversity not as destructive forces, but as transformative fires, propelling me towards constant evolution and growth.

Lead with Resilience (L): Through my experiences, resilience became my guiding light. I led with resilience, embracing struggles and victories alike, recognizing their power to shape me. Becoming a resilience mentor, I advocated for its transformative power in education. My journey from Liberia to America stands as a testament, inspiring others to overcome challenges.

Inspire Action (I): Throughout my journey, I've witnessed the transformative power of action. Learning the principles of Cognitive Behavioral Therapy (CBT) underscored the impact of thoughts on emotions and subsequent actions. Motivated by a deep desire to enact change, I transitioned from a passive observer to an engaged participant. By inspiring action, we become the architects of our lives, initiating a ripple effect that not only transforms us but also those in our sphere of influence.

Empower and Elevate (E): Empowerment was pivotal in my journey. Blessed with a grandmother and mother who instilled unwavering belief in my abilities, despite life's adversities, I recall my grandmother's words upon my acceptance to the University of Oklahoma, Tulsa: "I always knew you were meant for great things." Her belief fueled my aspirations to reach for the stars.

Nurture Well-being (N): My journey underscored the significance of nurturing mental and emotional well-being. Confronting trauma, loss, and stress profoundly affected my psychological health. Seeking help, I learned strategies to nurture my well-being, fostering resilience and equipping me to confront future challenges with strength.

Cultivate Growth (C): Every challenge presented an opportunity for growth. As a dedicated learner, I understood that each adversity held valuable lessons. My academic journey, spanning from Liberia to America, emphasized the importance of fostering growth irrespective of circumstances.

Envision the Promise (E): Envisioning a brighter future means holding steadfast to your goals, even amidst adversity. My vision of a better life fueled my resilience and determination. I vividly recall standing on the steps of the University of Oklahoma, Tulsa, clutching my Master's degree, surrounded by a cheering crowd of friends and family. In that triumphant moment, I realized my vision, overcoming countless adversities to reach this pinnacle of achievement.

With every step of the *RESILIENCE model*, I've walked a mile, carrying lessons from my past and the promise of a better future. By sharing this journey, I hope to inspire others, offering them a beacon to guide their paths and light their way toward resilience and empowerment.

As you traverse through "Lighting the Path," you'll come to appreciate the unique significance of each letter in *RESILIENCE*. Each represents a step in the journey toward overcoming adversity and fostering personal growth. Together, they form a roadmap, offering guidance for those navigating their unique paths, lighting the way toward resilience and empowerment.

In the uncharted territories of life, the *RESILIENCE model* stands as a guiding light. Through its principles, it serves as a beacon of hope, illuminating the path for those caught in their personal storms, providing a sense of direction amidst the chaos.

Together, let's take this journey. Let's light the path for others and leave our mark in this world, one life at a time. The promise of resilience awaits us, ready to transform every struggle into a story of triumph, every adversity into an opportunity for growth. Let's walk this path together. Let's light the path.

9

The Power of Pen

"THERE IS NO GREATER AGONY THAN BEARING AN UNTOLD STORY INSIDE YOU." – MAYA ANGELOU

The Power of Pen symbolizes more than mere metaphor in my memoir; it embodies the essence of the written word's ability to ignite change, instill courage, and foster resilience. Throughout my personal journey of evolution, I've unearthed the profound impact of storytelling in sculpting our narratives and forging connections with the world around us.

My tale commenced amidst the heartache of Liberia, where civil unrest had scarred the landscape. Our makeshift home nestled within dense jungles, forming the backdrop to the opening chapters of my life. It was within those jungle depths, beneath the relentless African sun, that a child's spirit learned to dream, to hope, and, above all, to persevere.

My pen emerged as my voice, a conduit through which I could articulate my experiences beyond the constraints of time and place.

From the war-torn streets of Monrovia to the vibrant cities of America, my narratives traversed continents and cultures. The pen, an extension of my very essence, etched the poignant symphony of my existence onto the canvas of time. Each page bore witness to tales of despair, perseverance, hope, and triumph, mapping the trajectory of my evolution.

Embarking on the daunting task of translating my life onto paper proved to be a profoundly cathartic journey. I confronted the relentless demand for vulnerability that memoir-writing imposes, peeling back the layers of strength to reveal the raw wounds of my past. Each memory resurrected felt like summoning ghosts from the depths of my soul. The echoes of gunfire piercing the African night, the relentless ache of hunger gnawing at our bellies, the searing agony of loss—all rushed back with a visceral intensity.

As I grappled with these haunting echoes of my past, I stumbled upon the profound catharsis that vulnerability brings. The art of storytelling revealed itself not just as a means to revisit my history, but as a pathway to healing—a key to unlocking the potential for self-understanding and transformation.

In "The Power of Pen," I aimed to encapsulate not only the tumultuous trajectory of my life but also the core of resilience threading through each chapter. Every word penned, every sentence crafted, stood as a testament to the indomitable spirit's determination to ascend from the depths of despair. Each paragraph chronicled the alchemy of transforming pain into power, adversity into strength, and trials into triumphs.

As my narrative unfurled upon the pages, I came to recognize storytelling as a powerful catalyst for personal evolution. With each word, each line, each page, I embarked on an internal metamorphosis. Every recalled memory became a stepping stone along the path of self-discovery, illuminating the contours of my identity, the depths of my struggles, and the heights of my triumphs.

The journey of memoir-writing also became an exploration of the intricate bond between the storyteller and the reader. The essence of storytelling lies in its capacity to evoke empathy, to forge connections between souls, and to remind us that, fundamentally, we are not alone in our struggles. Within this chapter, you will witness the profound impact of storytelling—not solely as a personal odyssey but as a universal bridge. Through the act of sharing our stories, we set forth a ripple effect, igniting courage in others to unveil their own narratives.

I firmly believe that our stories, much like ourselves, are in a perpetual state of evolution. They expand and adapt alongside us, reflecting our journey of growth and change. Through the act of penning down the chapters of my life, I unearthed the profound influence of storytelling as a catalyst for change. Our narratives possess the potential to serve as beacons of hope, casting light upon the road to resilience and transformation, not only for ourselves but also for those who discover solace and inspiration within our words.

In "The Power of Pen," I extend an invitation for you to embark on a journey alongside me, navigating through the complexities of my life's experiences as I bare my soul and recount the milestones of my journey. As we traverse these pages, you will observe how the art of storytelling emerged as a profound catalyst for my personal evolution and transformation. It is my hope that within these narratives, you will uncover the remarkable power that your own stories hold, inspiring reflection and growth within yourself.

As you journey deeper into this chapter, my wish is for you to discover inspiration and summon the courage to embrace your own stories. Remember, your narrative transcends mere recollection of past events. It stands as a testament to your resilience, a testament to the trials you've encountered and the triumphs you've attained. It's your distinctive imprint upon the canvas of the world, an expression of your individuality and strength.

As I reflect upon the path I've traversed, a wave of gratitude washes over me. It's been a journey spanning a thousand miles, marked by trials and triumphs alike, yet every step has been profoundly meaningful. Each stride has propelled me closer to self-discovery, revealing my inner strengths and shaping me into a beacon of hope for others to follow.

This memoir transcends mere chronicles of my past; it stands as a testament to the transformative force of storytelling and the unwavering resilience of the human spirit. Thus, I extend a heartfelt invitation to you, dear reader, to accompany me on this profound journey. Together, let us delve into the boundless power of the pen, exploring the potent magic of storytelling and the enduring strength of resilience that resides within each of us.

May we all learn to wield the power of the pen to inscribe our narratives, bear witness to our resilience, and inspire the world with our stories.

In Chapter 9, "The Power of Pen," I present to you a captivating and demanding voyage that has molded both myself and the world in which I dwell. This chapter transcends the mere craft of writing; it delves into the extraordinary odyssey of an individual—an immigrant, a student, a scholar—who unearthed the transformative potential of words to spark change.

As I grasped the pen for the initial time to inscribe my life's story, the endeavor loomed dauntingly before me. How could I hope to encapsulate the profundity of my experiences, the magnitude of the adversities surmounted, and the intensity of my metamorphosis? Each sentence seemed burdened with an immense responsibility. Yet, despite the weightiness of the task, I remained resolute and undeterred.

As I committed the initial words to paper, I sensed the floodgates of memory swinging open. The landscapes of my war-torn homeland, the resolute support of my family, the echoes of gunfire pierced by profound silence, the cultural disorientation of relocating to America, the unwavering pursuit of education, and the ensuing journey of personal evolution—all began to materialize, vivid and palpable, upon the page.

In my writing, I delved into the harrowing reality of war, capturing how it strips innocent children of their childhood, transforming their laughter into tears and their playgrounds into battlegrounds. I articulated the anguish of bidding farewell to my home, family, and friends, and embarking upon American soil, a tumultuous mix of hope and trepidation swirling within me. I chronicled my initial struggles with cultural disparities, language barriers, and academic hurdles, alongside the eventual triumph of finding my stride, forging enduring bonds, attaining academic milestones, and witnessing my own metamorphosis into a stronger, more resilient individual. My narrative traversed the trajectory from bewildered immigrant to impassioned mental health advocate—a journey marked by trials, triumphs, growth, and profound enlightenment.

Writing about these experiences stirred a torrent of emotions within me. The trauma of the past, the elation of small victories, the exhilaration of personal growth, and the pride of accomplishing my goals—all flooded into my narrative. With each stroke of the pen, as I transcribed my journey, I felt a profound sense of liberation. Writing became my catharsis, a means to release pent-up emotions, to reconcile with the past, and to embark on a journey of healing. It was as if every word flowing from my pen carried fragments of my pain, my struggles, my triumphs, and my transformation. The pen emerged as my confidant, my voice, my healer.

Crafting this memoir felt akin to navigating a pathway of self-discovery. Along the journey, I uncovered new dimensions of my character, uncharted territories of resilience, and a profound comprehension of my evolution. The act of writing served as both enlightenment and therapy. Gradually, I reframed my adversities not as impassable barriers but as stepping stones guiding me toward personal development and metamorphosis. No longer a passive bystander to circumstance, I emerged as an empowered architect of my destiny.

However, this chapter extends beyond my personal journey and transformation. It underscores the profound influence of storytelling in inspiring and catalyzing change. Every individual possesses a unique narrative, and each story holds the potential to strike a chord, ignite action, and instigate transformation. My tale of resilience and metamorphosis represents just one of countless narratives. Through the sharing of my story, my aspiration was to resonate with readers across the globe who may be grappling with their own adversities, seeking a glimmer of hope. I aimed to inspire them, to reassure them that they are not solitary in their struggles and that they too possess the capacity to turn their challenges into opportunities for growth.

"The Power of Pen" underscores the transformative potential of storytelling to cultivate connection, ignite empathy, and empower individuals. It highlights the indispensable role of narratives in destigmatizing mental health challenges, fostering resilience, and fostering open dialogue on these pressing issues. It advocates for the profound impact of words in inspiring, uplifting, and catalyzing change.

In this chapter, I implore you to seize your pen and commence the narration of your own story. Your singular narrative possesses the potential to act as a potent agent of change—not solely for yourself, but also for others who discover resonance in your words. Your story holds significance. Your voice holds sway. Therefore, let us embark together upon an exploration of the transformative might of storytelling. Let us traverse the realm where ink converges with paper, where silence discovers its voice, and where resilience finds its eloquent narration.

Remember, our past and present experiences serve as mere chapters in the grand tapestry of our life story. Our future lies as a blank page, poised to be adorned with our triumphs. Embrace the boundless potential of your pen and commence the authoring of your narrative of resilience. May our stories serve as beacons of inspiration, illuminating the paths of others and effecting positive change. Let us harness the formidable power of our pens to script a brighter future, both for ourselves and for the world at large.

10

The Promise Fulfilled

"THE FUTURE BELONGS TO THOSE WHO BELIEVE IN THE
BEAUTY OF THEIR DREAMS." – ELEANOR ROOSEVELT

With each successive page that unfolds the tapestry of my life's journey, I am drawn back into the rich spectrum of emotions that color my past. An intricate fusion of delight, agony, and eventual triumph, my journey stands as a testament to the unwavering resilience of the human spirit and its boundless capacity for transformation.

Let us journey back in time, to the turbulent landscape of my childhood in West Point, Liberia. Here, amid the chaos of a nation engulfed in conflict, the seeds of my resilience took root within the soil of my character. The disturbance of civil strife, the haunting specter of death, and the grim reality of a life overshadowed by unrest were my enduring companions.

In those formative years, every dawn heralded a test of survival, every passing day a relentless battle. Yet, amidst the tumultuous beginnings, my resilience was forged and fortified. Each sunrise further steeled my determination, imparting the profound lesson that even in the darkest of hours, the ember of hope could yet be ignited. It was during those early years that I mastered the art of seizing the fleeting moments of joy and hope that pierced through the veil of despair, holding them close to my heart as shields against the looming specter of hopelessness.

The subsequent chapter in my narrative unfolded thousands of miles away, upon foreign shores in the United States. Exchanging the chaotic streets of Liberia for the orderly lanes of America, the transition proved tumultuous. Maneuvering through an alien culture, understanding a foreign tongue, and grappling with an unfamiliar educational system, each day presented a battle on a fresh frontier. Yet, with each victory claimed, each obstacle surmounted, I move slowly to my aspiration—to transcend the constraints of my origin and craft a legacy capable of effecting change in the world.

Immersing myself wholeheartedly in the realm of psychology and mental health, I embarked on the journey of unraveling the intricate threads of my past. Each nugget of newfound knowledge served as a beacon, piercing through the darkness of my memories and bestowing fresh clarity upon experiences once shrouded in pain and confusion. The obstacles that I had once perceived as chains began to transmute into stepping-stones, paving the way for the transformative journey that led to my metamorphosis.

My journey led me through the corridors of Northeastern State University, the University of Oklahoma, and eventually to the hallways of CREOKS Behavioral Health Services. Here, I delved deep into the study and application of mental health counseling, a field that sparked an unrestrained passion within me. No longer a passive observer, I emerged as an active participant in the realm of mental health, where my own narrative intertwined with and was shaped by the stories of those I served.

As I contemplate the trajectory of my journey, I perceive the arc of transformation with striking clarity. I envision the silhouette of a man, once ensnared by the constraints of his circumstances, breaking the shackles of his past and embracing the boundless potential of self-determination. I witness a flicker of curiosity, sparked by adversity, nurtured by resilience, blossoming into an unwavering flame of passion and purpose. I observe the metamorphosis from a survivor navigating through trauma to a beacon of hope, casting a radiant light to guide others along their path to healing.

As I navigate through the numerous chapters of my life, a deep wellspring of gratitude floods my being. Gratitude for the trials that sculpted my character, the obstacles that fortified my resilience, the triumphs that reinforced my determination, and the ongoing transformation that shaped the tapestry of my narrative. Each reflection upon the past serves as a poignant reminder of the vast expanse I have traversed, propelling me ever onward on my journey of growth and self-discovery.

At every juncture of my journey, each milestone attained, and every setback transcended, I find myself propelled further along the path of evolution. From the tumult of Liberia to the structured realm of Oklahoma, from a troubled youth to a fervent mental health advocate, every stride of my journey has left an indelible mark on the narrative of my existence.

In recounting my journey, I aspire to strike a chord with others navigating their labyrinth of transformation. Through sharing my story, I endeavor to illuminate the profound potency of resilience and the limitless capacity for change inherent within each of us. By doing so, I aim to ignite a spark of inspiration in others as they embark on their paths toward healing and transformation. For within all of us lies the power to transform; all that is required is to seize it and embark on the adventure of a lifetime. Our narratives are not defined by our circumstances, but rather by how we rise above them and fashion them into stepping stones toward our aspirations. And within that transformation, we discover our true selves.

As I flip through the pages of my past, a mixture of images, emotions, and recollections drown my consciousness. Each one serves as a testament to a voyage adorned with joy, despair, adversity, triumph, and metamorphosis. A journey that has carried me from the ravaged streets of Liberia to the vibrant metropolises of the United States. A journey that has witnessed my evolution from a troubled youth into a dedicated mental health counselor. And as this journey persists, each footfall marks the origin of a fresh chapter in my life's narrative.

My story spread out amidst the slums of West Point, Liberia, a locale engraved with the wounds of civil strife and societal discord. Each street corner vibrates with the echoes of gunfire and anguished cries, while every façade bears the weathered lines of desperation and resilience. Days are shrouded in uncertainty, with every passing moment infused with an undercurrent of apprehension and dread.

Amidst the tumultuous chaos, my resilience took root. It multiplied from the fertile soil of adversity, nurtured by the harsh conditions of survival, and fortified by the relentless bursts of uncertainty. Here, amidst the debris and devastation, I mastered the art of adaptation, the tenacity to persevere, and the audacity to envision a future beyond the confines of my present reality.

As I matured, my life took an unforeseen route when I embarked on a journey to the United States. This transition was not merely a change in location but a profound shift encompassing cultural, social, and personal dimensions. Here I was, a teenager from a war-ravaged nation, thrust into a realm utterly foreign to me. The language differed, the customs were unfamiliar, and the expectations loomed dauntingly. Nevertheless, I confronted these trials with the same resilience that had sustained me in Liberia. Each obstacle, each stumble, served as a stepping-stone toward my aspiration—a dream of transcending my circumstances, of effecting change, and of inspiring transformation.

Amidst the adjustments to American life, I also plunged deeper into the realms of psychology and mental health. This journey resembled being handed a mirror, offering a profound reflection of myself for the first time. It felt akin to reading my own story, finally deciphering the chapters once shrouded in confusion and pain. What were once perceived as burdensome experiences now revealed themselves as catalysts for my transformation.

Education was a turning point for me. At Northeastern State University, the University of Oklahoma, and CREOKS Behavioral Health Services, I found my calling. These institutions were not just platforms for learning but served as launchpads for my career. My understanding of mental health was no longer confined to textbooks; it extended into real-life interactions, experiences, and transformations. Here, I discovered the power and potential of my role as a mental health counselor. I was not a passive observer in the world of mental health; I was an active participant, shaping, and being shaped by the stories of those I served.

Now, as I cast my gaze backward, I behold a tapestry interwoven with threads of hope and optimism. I witness the young boy who once resigned himself to the belief that his circumstances dictated his fate, evolving into a man who realized he possessed the power to shape his own destiny. I observe the spark of curiosity burgeoning into a fervent flame of passion. I witness the evolution from a mere survivor to a radiant beacon of hope for others.

As I reflect upon my journey, my heart overflows with gratitude. I am thankful for the experiences that shaped me, the challenges that tested my resilience, the triumphs that fueled my determination, and the transformative moments that sculpted my path. With each glance backward, I am reminded of the vast distance I have traversed and find renewed vigor to forge ahead. Each remembrance serves as a poignant testament to my ongoing evolution, and I hope it may inspire others in their own journeys of transformation.

As I commit these words to paper, I am not merely recounting my past; I am crafting the blueprint for my future. I am presenting a narrative steeped in resilience, courage, and transformation, one that I aspire will strike a chord with others and kindle within them the desire to embark on their own odysseys of self-discovery and personal growth. I eagerly anticipate the continuation of this journey—of learning, evolving, and metamorphosing. I am prepared to embrace the challenges and triumphs that lie ahead with unwavering resilience, graceful resolve, and an enduring spirit of hope.

From the depths of the slums in Liberia to the vibrant community of Oklahoma, my story stands as a testament to the indomitable power of human resilience and the boundless potential for transformation. My journey serves as a poignant reminder that while our past experiences may shape us, they need not define us. Adversity, far from being a barrier, can serve as a potent catalyst for profound change. It underscores the universal truth that each of us possesses the inherent capacity to rewrite the script of our lives and to positively impact the lives of those around us.

As I persist on my journey through life, I remain acutely aware of the enduring potency of resilience, the unwavering fortitude of the human spirit, and the transformative influence of hope. These invaluable lessons, far from being relegated to my past, serve as steadfast guideposts illuminating the path forward. They are the threads that intricately connect the chapters of my existence, weaving together the narrative of my ongoing journey.

Looking into the horizon, I am filled with anticipation for what lies ahead. I am eager to persist in my mission of supporting individuals grappling with mental health challenges. To ignite inspiration in others through the telling of my story. And to persistently push the limits of what can be achieved. If there is one profound lesson collected from my journey, it is the realization of our collective capacity for extraordinary feats. We need only to cultivate belief in ourselves, embrace our inherent resilience, and remain open to the transformative power of change.

As I conclude this chapter of my life and stand on the height of writing the next, I do so infused with anticipation, optimism, and an unwavering faith in the strength of resilience. The blank pages of my future stretch before me, pregnant with possibility. Possibility for growth, for metamorphosis, for effecting change. And I stand poised, ready to embrace every opportunity that lies ahead with open arms.

WORDS OF WISDOM

This memoir, the story intricately woven throughout its pages, is distinctly mine. It bears my fingerprints, my tears, my laughter, and my growth. However, I am acutely aware that I am not alone on this journey. Countless other young men and women trace their lines of hardship and carve their unique narratives of resilience. This tale is about a boy who stumbled, who fell, who bore the dirt and grit of life's challenges. Yet, he refused to bow to adversity. Instead, he rose, transformed, and extended a guiding hand to others who were still finding their footing.

In the garden of life, I've sown seeds of mistakes and reaped my harvest of challenges. Yet, these were never my definitions. They could not dim the shining glow of my hope. I have observed the world through the lens of a pessimist. Every misstep, every challenge, becomes a reflection of their worth. The echoes of self-deprecating thoughts such as 'I'm no good. I can't do better. Things won't change,' drown the whispers of hope. This mindset stifles ambition, quashes initiative, and leaves a barren field where the seeds of growth could have thrived.

Here is my hard-earned wisdom. An optimist does not draw back from trials. They confront their challenges, acknowledging that certain circumstances may be beyond their control, yet they refuse to let these circumstances seize their destiny. They reflect on their past, seize the opportunities that lie before them, and persist with relentless determination. Their fuel is a purpose, a blazing beacon that guides their journey. Be it a commitment to causing change or unwavering dedication to righteousness, this purpose propels them forward. Change is not seen as an adversary but as an ally, the hammer and chisel that shape their masterpiece of triumph. That triumph, in turn, fuels their desire to elevate others.

Embracing optimism and anchoring my journey to the float of hope has navigated me through the profound waters of mental health. This choice inspired me to document my experiences—the lows and the highs, my transformation and victories, my unwavering dedication—all penned with a single purpose: to inspire and empower you. No matter the shadows that linger from your past or the turbulent storms you find yourself battling now, know that they do not define your essence. They serve as stepping-stones on your path to success.

Hold fast to hope; let it be the force that transforms your struggles into the momentum propelling you forward. Evolve, triumph, and extend your hand to make a lasting impact, both in your life and in the lives of others. This message, this heartfelt plea, this promise, is my gift to you. To capture this sentiment, I invoke the words of Winston Churchill: "We make a living by what we get, but we make a life by what we give." This quote not only melds seamlessly into the tapestry of my narrative but also amplifies the essence of our shared human journey—to give, to inspire, and to empower.

11

The Journey Continues

> "THE ONLY THING THAT STANDS BETWEEN YOU AND YOUR DREAM IS THE WILL TO TRY AND THE BELIEF THAT IT IS ACTUALLY POSSIBLE."– JOEL BROWN

As we embark upon the final section of this memoir, we stand at a juncture that marks both a culmination and a new beginning. Here, we pause, allowing ourselves a moment of reflection as we cast our gaze back upon the winding path we've traversed. It is a journey marked by adversity and struggle, yet undeniably magnificent in its lessons of resilience.

From the echoes of my childhood to the turmoil of wars, from the loss of dear ones to the unfamiliarity of new shores, each event and emotion has etched a permanent imprint on my story. I journeyed through the fires of life, bearing the weight of every hardship and the resilience forged in each battle. Yet, amidst the ashes and the smokescreen of challenges, I did not emerge as a victim of circumstances but as the victor of my narrative.

My story is a testament to the *RESILIENCE model*, a practical blueprint to not only weather the storms of life but to harness their winds and chart a course toward brighter horizons. Each step of this model, from Recognizing the Journey to Envisioning the Promise, is a chapter of my own life, each experience an illustration of its principles.

As we approach the conclusion of this narrative, it's crucial to recognize that this is not the finale of my journey; instead, it signifies a promising new beginning. Life will persist in its unfolding, presenting fresh challenges and victories alike. However, the tapestry of my story is forever woven with the threads of resilience, optimism, and an unwavering dedication to transformation.

As I gaze toward the future, my hopes and aspirations are centered on nurturing leaders who embody not only competence and intelligence, but also resilience, emotional fortitude, and a profound readiness to effect meaningful change. The path that lies ahead brims with promise, and I extend a heartfelt invitation to you, dear reader, to journey onward with me. Together, let us continue walking towards a brighter tomorrow.

Because the journey doesn't conclude here. It unfolds continuously. Within this ongoing odyssey, we discover not merely the narrative of one individual's resilience, but a universal anthem resonating with hope, transformation, and the triumph over adversity. This is the melody of resilience, the symphony of life, and I am profoundly grateful to have you as a vital part of it. As we part ways, I leave you with these poignant words of President Franklin D. Roosevelt, which summarize the essence of the journey we've shared within the pages of this memoir: "The only limit to our realization of tomorrow will be our doubts of today."

Conclusion

As I stand at the face of this extraordinary journey, a tapestry of intricate emotions develops within me. The past, vivid with pain, resilience, joy, and transformation, intertwines with a present filled with gratitude, and a future humming with hopeful anticipation. Each page of this memoir serves as a testament to the journey I've undertaken—a walk adorned with daunting adversities and awe-inspiring triumphs, a visit both personal and universal.

Reflecting on my origins, my journey commenced amidst the tumultuous backdrop of West Point, Liberia—a place where childhood innocence was suffocated by the icy grip of war, and survival was not assured but rather a relentless daily battle. It was within this discord of chaos that I first glimpsed the transformative power of resilience—an insight that would serve as a guiding light through the darkest passages of my life.

The journey then led me to the United States, a land brimming with promises of dreams but also laden with its own set of trials. Confronting a new culture, grappling with an unfamiliar tongue, and navigating the labyrinth of an alien education system, my resilience was incessantly put to the test. However, with each tribulation encountered and every stumble endured, I found myself propelled further toward my ambition—to transcend the constraints life had imposed and carve a meaningful mark upon the world.

My exploration into the realms of psychology and mental health opened up new dimensions of understanding. It was as if I were unraveling the intricacies of my own narrative, bringing clarity to chapters once clouded by confusion and anguish. The burdens I once carried transformed into potent catalysts fueling my metamorphosis—a transformation that shaped me, refined me, and ultimately, led to my rebirth.

Within the halls of Northeastern State University, the University of Oklahoma, and CREOKS, I transitioned from a mere observer to an active change-maker within the mental health sphere. Immersed in countless tales of human suffering and resilience, my narrative acquired a deeper significance. It ceased to be solely about me; instead, it became a beacon of hope—a testament to the indomitable capacity of the human spirit to withstand, adapt, and thrive.

Now, as I pen down these concluding lines, a profound sense of gratitude washes over me. Gratitude for the trials that molded me, the triumphs that uplifted me, the metamorphosis that defined me. Every step of this voyage stands as an emblem of the invincible power of resilience, the endurance of the human spirit, and the limitless potential for change that resides within each of us.

As I peer into the horizon of the future, hope washes over me like a gentle tide. I am filled with aspiration to persist in my journey within the realm of mental health counseling, walking alongside others on their paths toward self-discovery, healing, and growth. My desire is to keep weaving the threads of my story, with the hope that it may serve as a source of inspiration for others to confront their own narratives and catalyze their unique transformations. I am eager to embrace the ongoing evolution of my life, welcoming its serendipitous moments and bravely navigating its stormy seas with resolve and courage.

As you, dear reader, arrive at the culmination of this memoir, my heartfelt wish is for you to be stirred—to awaken to your resilience, to unearth the depths of your inner strength, and to realize the boundless potential for transformation that resides within you. Each of us is capable of remarkable feats. All it takes is unwavering resilience, a sprinkle of courage, and a steadfast belief in ourselves.

As I gently set down my pen and draw the curtains on this chapter of my existence, I do so with a heart brimming with gratitude and a spirit ablaze with anticipation. This memoir stands as a monument to my journey—a hymn of praise for resilience and a testament to the transformative power of the human spirit. I hope that it serves as a beacon of hope, a catalyst for introspection, and a gentle reminder of the formidable resilience nestled within each of us.

Indeed, let us remember that our narratives are ever-evolving, our journeys far from reaching their conclusion. With the pen firmly in our grasp and the future as our blank canvas, we have the power to script our odysseys. As we embark upon this creative endeavor, let us infuse our narratives with courage, resilience, and unwavering hope. And when we glance back upon the chapters we've written, may it be with a sense of pride and conviction—for we have not merely survived, but we have thrived, blossomed, and undergone a profound transformation.

As one chapter draws to a close, another eagerly awaits its commencement, radiant with possibilities and teeming with opportunities for further growth. As the wheel of time ceaselessly turns, I will persist in chronicling my story—a narrative woven with threads of resilience, hope, and perpetual evolution. As I continue on this journey, I earnestly hope that you, too, will take up your pen and embark upon your next chapter. For our stories are not mere echoes of the past; they are the blueprints of our future. They stand as enduring testaments to our inherent resilience and our indomitable spirit of transformation.

Thank you, dear reader, for embarking on this journey with me, resonating with my story, and finding fragments of your narrative within mine. As you close this book, I hope you carry with you a renewed sense of resilience, a deep-seated belief in your capacity to transform, and an unquenchable thirst to craft your exceptional narrative, all inspired by 'The Unbreakable Human Spirit of Resilience.'

Epilogue

Years have passed since I embarked on my journey from the humble, dust-laden streets of West Point to the shores of opportunities that lay beyond. Each day has been a testament to the resilience instilled within me by the trials and tribulations of my past, and every challenge overcome, a tribute to the enduring spirit of my people.

In the panorama of my life, Liberia remains a vivid, heartrending backdrop, an intricate tapestry of suffering and triumph, despair, and hope. My roots run deep into its soil, drawing strength from the land's resilience, and my spirit soars high into its azure skies, carrying with it the dreams and aspirations of its people.

Life has been an unending voyage of discovery. The world beyond West Point was vast, laden with challenges, and filled with opportunities. Some trials shook me, and triumphs shaped me, each an integral part of the odyssey that brought me where I am today. The spirit of West Point, the unyielding resilience, the camaraderie, and the indefatigable will to survive were my guiding stars, illuminating my path in the darkest of nights.

I realize now that West Point was more than just a place; it was a crucible that forged the essence of my being. The resilience, the courage, the spirit to strive and survive, and the lessons learned on those bustling streets, and within the warm confines of our communal home, have been the compass guiding me through life's labyrinth.

As I pen these concluding words, I am filled with profound gratitude. Gratitude for the trials that honed me, for the lessons that guided me, for the love that nurtured me, and for the opportunity to share my story with the world.

The saga of West Point, the tale of Liberia, is far from over. It is an ongoing narrative, a testament to the strong spirit of humanity that rises above adversity and seeks hope midst of despair. As we forge ahead into a future laden with uncertainties, let us carry with us the lessons from our past and the spirit of resilience that defines us.

In the end, our lives are but tales woven into the vast tapestry of human existence, each thread adding depth and richness to the grand narrative. May the tale of my journey from the streets of West Point to beyond, serve as a beacon of hope for those navigating through the stormy seas of adversity.

After all, if you make it out of West Point, you can make it anywhere. And it is this belief, this unshakable faith, that lights my path toward a brighter, more hopeful tomorrow. As I look back on the journey that has been, and ahead at the path that is yet to unfold, I am reminded of a simple, yet profound truth — our pasts shape us, but they do not define us. The future is yet to be written, and in our hands, we hold the pen. So, let us write a tale worth telling, a tale of resilience, hope, and an unfading dream of liberty.

Afterword

As I pen this concluding segment of my memoir, I find myself reflecting on the journey that has led to this point. The process of writing my story has been a transformative one, offering a platform for introspection, acceptance, and growth, much like the tale it narrates.

Writing 'The Unbreakable Human Spirit of Resilience' has been more than just recounting my life's experiences; it has been a journey of healing and a testament to the resilience that lies within us all. I hope that the readers who have accompanied me on this journey have been inspired by it and find the courage within themselves to confront their own adversities head-on.

The creation of this memoir, from the first words jotted down in a quiet moment of reflection, to the final edits made in anticipation of its release, has taught me the power of words and the impact they can have. It has taught me that our stories are not just our own but belong to the collective human experience. They have the power to inspire, to heal, and to foster understanding and empathy in ways nothing else can.

As I look back at the journey I've taken, not just in the pages of this book, but in my life, I see how far I've come, and how each challenge, each setback, and each victory, has contributed to the person I am today. I hope that this memoir has managed to convey that each one of us is capable of such transformation.

Since the completion of this memoir, my journey has continued to unfold, with new challenges, discoveries, and lessons learned. The resilience that I've developed over the years continues to serve me, just as I hope it will serve you, dear reader, in your journeys.

If there's one thing, I'd like you to take away from this book, it's the understanding that no matter the adversities we face, we possess the power to transcend them. We are the authors of our own stories, capable of transforming our narratives into testimonies of strength, courage, and resilience.

And so, as we conclude this chapter, remember that your story is still being written. Let it be a testament to your resilience, a reflection of your strength, and a beacon of hope for others. Continue to grow, learn, and share your story, for the world needs to hear it.

I want to express my deepest gratitude to you, dear reader, for journeying with me. Your companionship on this voyage has made every word worthwhile. Thank you for allowing me to share my story, and for finding a place for it in your heart.

Here's to The Unbreakable Human Spirit of Resilience.

Acknowledgements

To my precious wife, Mrs. Pheona Ketter, my steadfast partner in life's journey. You've been with me from the start, your unwavering support and wisdom a guiding light in the pursuit of my dreams. Your belief in me has been my stronghold, your love, my sanctuary. I love you, now and always.

To my beloved mother, Mrs. Doris Tamba Ayeni, I am profoundly grateful for your unwavering love, guidance, and sacrifice that have shaped me into the person I am today. Your resilience and strength are the bedrock of my own, inspiring me to face life's challenges with courage and grace. Thank you for being my constant source of support and for instilling in me the values that guide my path. Your influence is immeasurable, and I am eternally grateful.

To my dad, Mr. McDonald Ayeni, you have played a profound role in my life. You were the first person I proudly called 'Dad' because that is who you truly are to me. Your presence has brought stability, love, and guidance that have been indispensable. You have taught me the meaning of integrity, hard work, and compassion. Thank you for embracing me as your own and for being an incredible father figure.

To my younger sister, Katherine Ketter, your unwavering support has been a pillar in my life. Your faith in me and your relentless encouragement have propelled me forward, fueling my journey and aspirations. Our bond stands as a testament to profound strength and joy, your influence reaching beyond me to grace my children with your warmth and kindness. I am grateful for your role as my confidante, my champion, and the cherished aunt to my children. Your presence is a treasure I hold dear. I also extend my heartfelt thanks to my sister, Siah Tamba, for capturing images from our childhood home on "The Rock," which have been instrumental in this memoir. Your assistance is deeply appreciated.

A heartfelt thanks to my father, Mr. Amos James Ketter, my stepmother, Patience Ketter, my aunt, Ms. Siah Karloh, and all my uncles, aunts, and family from "The Rock." Your unwavering love and support have shaped me into the resilient individual I am today. Your guidance and nurturing have instilled within me the strength to navigate life's challenges, and for that, I am forever grateful.

To my spiritual father, Rev. Dr. Wisdom Okotie, his dear wife Rev. Theresa Okotie, and the entire family of Christ the King Miracle Church. Your ceaseless support, prayers, and acceptance have meant more than words can express. The church offered me a sanctuary, a place to call home, and for this, my heart overflowed with gratitude. You have all been instrumental in shaping the man I am today, and for that, I am eternally thankful.

To my dear daughter, Noelle Kumba Ketter, our unexpected blessing, you sparked the inspiration for this memoir in moments of tranquility, cradled in my arms under the moonlit sky. Your arrival, a delightful surprise, breathed new life into our family narrative, guiding me to explore and document our story. You, Noelle, have been the muse behind this journey of reflection, and for that, I am immensely thankful. To Noah, Nathan, Naomi, and Nehemiah, each of you fills my life with joy and purpose. You are the heart of my world, the essence of my identity as a father.

Finally, I am deeply grateful to my Board Approved Supervisor, Brian Ormsby, LPC-S, thank you for believing in me and making my time with you worth it. I learned so much from you and because of your insights, I have become a knowledgeable mental health counselor and continue to harness my skills.

Index

- Africa, Continent of — p. xi
- American Dream, pursuit of — pp. 113, 114
- Boarding School, Mission — pp. 40, 46
- Discipline and Hardships — p. 48
- Quest to Save a Troubled Child — p. 42
- Civil War, Liberian — pp. 60, 61
- Community, Spirit of — pp. 2, 19, 20
- Cultural Shifts, navigating — p. 81
- Education, journey in — pp. 40, 71
- Empowerment, Promise of — p. 157
- Family, Dynamics — p. 56
- Hope, Journey to — p. 78
- Liberia — pp. xi, xiii, 13, 14, 15
- Mental Health, exploration of — p. 143
- Mission Boarding School — pp. 40, 46
- Mamba Point — p. 19
- Paynesville, significance of — pp. 57, 58
- Personal Growth and Transformation — pp. 102, 131
- Resilience - throughout the document — pp. 1, 147, 153
- Second Liberian Civil War, impact of — pp. 60, 61
- The Rock, descriptions and memories — pp. 34, 35
- Transformation, Power of — pp. 102, 131
- United States, adapting to life in — pp. 81, 82
- Unity and Strength, themes of — pp. 56, 57
- West Point — pp. 2, 13, 14

Notes

Notes to Chapter 1: The Echoes of Childhood

- Notes: Introduces the author's early life in West Point, focusing on the vibrant yet challenging environment that shaped his early years, including the influence of his grandparents.

Notes to Chapter 2: Under the Shadow of War

- Notes: Details the impact of the Liberian Civil War on the author and his community, highlighting the fear, loss, and resilience that characterized this period.

Notes to Chapter 3: A New Dawn

- Notes: Describes the aftermath of the war and the beginning of recovery, emphasizing the author's personal and family efforts to rebuild their lives amidst continuing challenges.

Notes to Chapter 4: The Guiding Light

- Notes: Focuses on pivotal moments and individuals that provided guidance and hope to the author, aiding his journey towards healing and growth.

Notes to Chapter 5: Turning Pages

- Notes: Chronicles the author's experiences with education and self-discovery, marking the beginning of a transformative journey through learning and reflection.

Notes to Chapter 6: The Seed of Change

- Notes: Explores significant personal developments and the gradual shift in the author's perspective and aspirations, leading to a renewed sense of purpose.

Notes to Chapter 7: Rising from the Ashes

- Notes: Highlights the author's achievements and milestones in the face of adversity, underscoring the unyielding nature of human resilience.

Notes to Chapter 8: Lighting the Path

- Notes: Reflects on the lessons learned and wisdom gained through hardship, and how these insights serve to illuminate the path forward for the author and others.

Notes to Chapter 9: The Power of Pen

- Notes: Discusses the author's discovery of writing as a powerful tool for expression, healing, and connecting with others, emphasizing its role in empowerment.

Notes to Chapter 10: The Promise Fulfilled

- Notes: Narrates the fulfillment of goals and dreams, showcasing the realization of the author's potential and the impact of his work on the wider community.

Notes to Chapter 11: The Journey Continues

- Notes: Concludes with a look towards the future, acknowledging ongoing challenges and the continuous journey of learning, growth, and advocacy for change.

References

American Psychological Association. (2019). Building your resilience. APA. https://www.apa.org/topics/resilience

BBC News Africa. (2002). Liberia ends state of emergency. BBC News. http://news.bbc.co.uk/2/hi/africa/2260112.stm

Encyclopedia.com (n.d.). Charles Taylor 1948–. In Encyclopedia.com. Retrieved July 29, 2023, from https://www.encyclopedia.com/education/news-wires-white-papers-and-books/taylor-charles-1948

Ginsburg, K. R. (2011). Building resilience in children and teens: Giving kids roots and wings. American Academy of Pediatrics.

Kieh, G. K., Jr. (2009). The Roots of the Second Liberian Civil War. International Journal on World Peace, 26(1), 7-30. Retrieved from https://www.jstor.org/stable/20752871

Kazdin, A. E. (2013). Behavior modification in applied settings. Waveland Press.

Rutter, M. (1985). Resilience in the face of adversity: Protective factors and resistance to psychiatric disorder. The British journal of psychiatry, 147(6), 598-611.

Seligman, M. E. P. (1998). Learned Optimism: How to Change Your Mind and Your Life. Vintage.

 Desmond Eric Ketter is a dedicated behavioral health practitioner with years of personal and professional experience in mental health. He is devoted to guiding children, teenagers, and young adults through the complexities of mental and emotional wellness as a licensed professional counselor. He earned a Bachelor of Science degree in Psychology, with a minor in Social Welfare, from Northeastern State University, and holds a Master's degree in Clinical Mental Health Counseling from the University of Oklahoma. Beyond his professional life, Desmond is married to Pheona, and together they have five incredible children. Additionally, he is the vice president of the Liberian Community Association of Tulsa and serves as an elder and youth coordinator at his local church, where he has been a committed member for over a decade.

You can connect with me on:
Website: https://desmondketter.com
Twitter: https://twitter.com/desmondketter
Facebook: https://www.facebook.com/desmond.ketter.9
Instagram: https://www.instagram.com/desmondericketter
TikTok: https://www.tiktok.com/@desmond_eric_ketter1

Stay Connected
Scan the QR code to leave a review, follow my updates, discover new books, and find out about upcoming events and specials. Your engagement means the world to me—thank you for being part of our community!

www.ingramcontent.com/pod-product-compliance
Lightning Source LLC
Chambersburg PA
CBHW030334010526
44119CB00028B/397/J